TAKING STOCK

OVER 75 YEARS OF THE OXO CUBE

ISSUED BY BROOKE BOND OXO LTD
TO COMMEMORATE THE DIAMOND JUBILEE OF THE OXO CUBE

Penny Vincenzi

Willow Books
Collins, 8 Grafton Street, London W1
1985

PHOTOGRAPHIC ACKNOWLEDGEMENTS

The publishers, author and Brooke Bond Oxo Ltd would like to thank the following sources for photographs in this book:

Bill Hill, Ad Search 17 (top), 31, 32, 33, 35, 36, 37, 65, 66, 67, 68, 69, 72, 73, 74, 75, 101; Robert Opie Collection 26, 56; James Haworth Ltd 27, 42 (bottom), 43, 45 (top), 50 (left), 78 (left), 80, 88 (left), 89 (bottom); Kodak Ltd 35; Debenhams plc 36 (left); Lotus Ltd 36 (top right); Paul Popper Ltd 62, 68, 70, 99, 100, 103, 104; The Marconi Company 65; British Railways Board 66; Radio Times 69; Weidenfeld & Nicolson 69; Syndication International Ltd 72; Ouzledale Foundry Co Ltd 74 (left); Hoover plc 74 (right); Frigidaire 75; The Press Association 83 (bottom); Austin Rover 101; JVC (UK) Ltd 102; Camera Press Ltd 105; British Gas 107 (top); Philips Electronics, 107 (bottom).

Willow Books
William Collins Sons & Co Ltd
London · Glasgow · Sydney
Auckland · Toronto · Johannesburg

First published in Great Britain 1985
© Brooke Bond Oxo Ltd/Collins Willow

Vincenzi, Penny
Taking stock.
1. Great Britain–Social life and customs–20th century
I. Title
941.082 DA566.4

ISBN 0 00 218157 6 (hardback)
ISBN 0 00 218165 7 (limpback)

Filmset by Wyvern Typesetting Ltd, Bristol

Printed in Great Britain by
William Collins Sons & Co Ltd, Glasgow

TAKING
STOCK

CONTENTS

BEFORE 1910

ONCE UPON A TIME

T HE Oxo cube was born, not as a cube and not as a cooking aid, but as a liquid. Its virtues were extolled by such diverse characters as Florence Nightingale, the second Duke of Wellington and Sir Henry Stanley, the explorer, all of whom recognized it as an aid to health and strength.

Oxo was invented by a chemist called Justus Liebig, whose history reads like a fairy story. Born in 1803, the son of a poor paint and colour manufacturer in a little German town, he was a dunce at school (although he did have a photographic memory and a passion for chemistry) to the despair of his family. Apprenticed later to a scientist, he was soon dismissed for blowing out all the windows of his employer's house in an early experiment. However, he quickly proved his brilliance and by the age of twenty he was a Doctor of Philosophy, given a grant by the Grand Duke of Hesse to continue his studies. He studied under the finest scientists in Paris and became a Professor at the University of Geissen. He was one of the great pioneers of science, and his methods of organic chemistry are still used. A barony was conferred upon him for his work in this field.

Liebig became an expert on human physiology, among other things, and the chemistry and classification of food, and wrote what can be seen as a prophetic paper on the dangers of boiling meat and destroying its goodness. During

Inventor of the Extract: Baron Justus von Liebig.

the 1840s, which were known as the 'hungry Forties', Liebig developed a concentrated extract of meat, to provide a substitute for the real thing for those unable to afford it, and to act as a substitute for beef tea. Little did he dream that nearly 150 years later a descendant of his product was to be as inevitable a part of virtually every kitchen as condiments. History was in the making; Oxo, or rather an early ancestor of it, had been born.

TAKING OFF

The product was so successful that many doctors wrote to Liebig, asking for his meat extract, and he wasn't able to meet the supply. He seized upon a scheme to make use of the huge surplus of meat in South America where cattle were slain purely for their hides and then discarded, offering his assistance to anyone who would work with him on this project, and his name to help sell the result. In 1861 a young engineer called George Christian Giebert read of Liebig's work and wrote to him, suggesting that they should meet to discuss a manufacturing plant in Uruguay. Liebig had found his protégé, and a way of reaching his dream of feeding the undernourished millions in Europe. Plans went ahead for the factory to be built in a small town called Fray Bentos on the banks of the Uruguay where cattle could be bought very cheaply. Extractum Carnis Liebig, as it was now called, looked set fair for a great future.

Spreading the word: an early advert for Liebig's meat extract.

ENGLISH TRANSLATION

Liebig's Extract came to England in 1865, and was marketed throughout the country, promoted as being invaluable not only in the sick-room but also in the kitchen. Its commercial value soared; it was advertised in the growing number of women's magazines and promoted in every recipe in a cookery book written by the German equivalent of Mrs Beeton.

Towards the end of the 19th century, many charming advertisements for Oxo appeared,

First of many firsts: Liebig's *Practical Cookery Book*, an early premium offer, free to all subscribers.

with much of the copy in verse, showing early Superwomen, all talented and capable cooks, using vast quantities of Extract.

Cooking's no more a worry,
When every cook can find
A stock that in a hurry,
Can suit the daintiest mind.
No weary, weary boiling,
Does Liebig's Extract need,
She fears no heat, no toiling,
Who Liebig's rules will heed.

Liebig's advertising was charming, persuasive – and extremely successful.

LIEBIG "COMPANY'S"
EXTRACT OF BEEF.

COOKERY BOOKS (indispensable for Ladies) sent FREE on application to

LIEBIG'S EXTRACT OF MEAT COMPANY, LTD.

9, FENCHURCH AVENUE, E.C.

An exhibition display-stand demonstrating that Liebig's manufacturing plant was at Fray Bentos in Uruguay.

AMONG THE SOUVENIRS

Oxo has always produced advertising material which is of such style and charm that it inevitably becomes memorabilia. During the 1890s and onwards the Company put out a huge selection of promotional items. There was a range of coloured lithographic menu cards on display in hotels and restaurants all over the country, educational and slightly ponderous in tone; the subject matter ranged from the Crowned Heads of Europe to the Reign of Queen Victoria. There were also chromos, rather like cigarette cards, given in exchange for labels or wrappers from pots of extract; decorative billheads; and silk bookmarks given to leading chemists and hospitals.

Pop goes the Extract:
early pop-up books
were used
in advertising.

Marketing turned
memorabilia: Liebig's
promotional offers,
such as coronation
souvenirs, sold the
product at the time
and have increased in
value ever since.

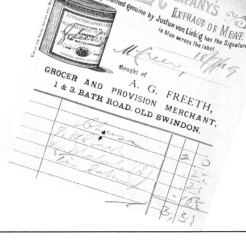

ABOVE
Chromos (coloured cards) were given in exchange for
labels or wrappers from pots of Extract.

RIGHT
A Liebig Company's bill-head.

One of the Liebig Company's lithographic menu cards.

ETHICAL MATTERS

The Extract's ethical value in the medical field was still considerable, too. It had Liebig's name, with its lofty associations, to lend it authenticity; it was extolled in the *Lancet* and other medical journals and many family doctors prescribed it. It was during this phase in its history that it received the praise from Florence Nightingale and the second Duke of Wellington, and the now famous jar accompanied Stanley on his historic 1865 expedition to find Dr Livingstone. A dramatic picture of Liebig's Extract being given to an ailing Madi carrier appeared in Stanley's account of the expedition.

Baron Von Liebig died in 1873, a much revered man. A statue to his memory was erected in Munich and portraits of him were painted in large numbers.

Dr Stanley, we presume: Liebig's Extract accompanied him every step of the way through 'darkest Africa' in search of Dr Livingstone.

ABOVE
The lady with the lamp and the Extract: Florence Nightingale at work in the hospital at Scutari.

RIGHT
Miss Nightingale's letter of praise to the Liebig Company.

EXTRACTUM BY ANY OTHER NAME

Liebig's Extract became Oxo in 1899. Strange though it may seem, the fact is that nobody has a very clear idea how the name came about. One legend (with no apparent factual basis) is that while a crate of the extract was at the docks a keen docker chalked O-X-O on the side to distinguish it from other cargo. The story might be true, because it was certainly a name that was very familiar at the depots. Whatever Oxo's origins, it was registered in 1899 as a trade mark everywhere in Europe, though not until June 1900 in Britain. It is certainly hard to imagine how a name could be slicker, neater and more easily engraved upon a public consciousness, nor more of a gift to graphic designers and advertising copywriters.

The famous name on the famous jar: an early sighting of the newly-christened Extract.

BACKBONE OF THE EMPIRE

At first Oxo was simply offered by the salesmen as a sideline to the original extract. But orders soon multiplied and the British public took the product to their hearts. Before long Oxo was being sold at station buffets, race-courses and agricultural shows. People were assured they would get their Oxo everywhere, and the enamel signs telling them so, beloved of collectors, are still up on some railway platforms.

PROMOTION

In 1902, the first Oxo promotional gift was given away: a baby's rattle with a handle that spelt Oxo was offered in exchange for a bottle-wrapper. In 1903 the name Oxo was beamed from an electric sign in the Strand. Another kind of innovative promotion was sponsorship. Oxo made itself synonymous with health, strength and endurance by the brilliantly simple device of sponsoring athletic events, such as the London to Brighton walk. The Company was not only official caterers at the 1908 London Olympics, supplying the runners in the marathon with drinks of Oxo to sustain them, but also managed to persuade the entire British team of athletes to recommend the product.

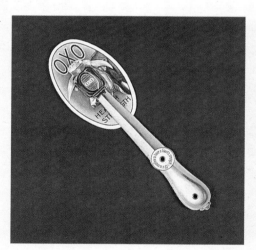

TOP AND OVERLEAF
Oxo soon became synonymous with health and fitness.

ABOVE LEFT AND RIGHT
Cutting their teeth on Oxo: a baby's rattle and picture book.

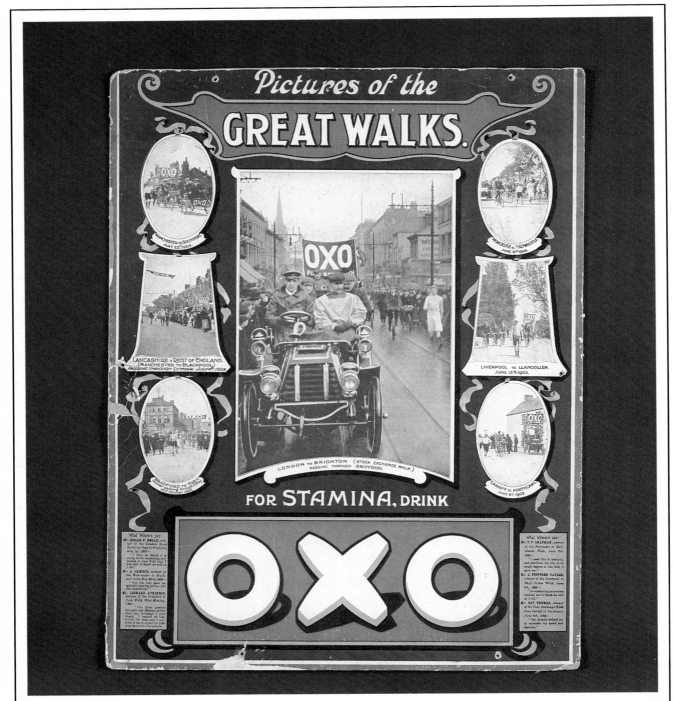

The Oxo Olympians: Oxo was official caterer to the 1908 London Olympics, and the entire British team endorsed the product.

WOMEN'S WORK

Perhaps most revolutionary of all, in 1902 the company decided to employ female labour. However, lest unseemly liaisons might take place over the bottling plants, it was laid down as part of the new arrangements that the ladies were located in a separate department with a different entrance from the men.

RIGHT
The Oxo female staff on an outing in 1909.

BELOW
Philanthropy, Oxo style: Blackpool police handed out liquid Oxo to poor children in 1909.

Blackpool Police
Distribution of
OXO
To the Poor Children of Blackpool
January 1909

THE END OF THE BEGINNING

Towards the end of this period, a more serious anxiety began to rear its head – the quality of the product. However delicious and beneficial Oxo might be, it left an unappetizing sediment in the bottom of the cup or bowl. Highly qualified chemists were set to work on the problem and perhaps in the process to discover a way of decreasing the price because a 2-ounce bottle of fluid Oxo was way beyond the means of the families who needed it most. A scheme was proposed for selling Oxo in capsules, and a short time later Liebig's chief chemist was given absolute control to pursue a 'penny product'. He did it. Nobody knows quite how. But beef essence and beef fibrine were fed into a Swiss cube-making machine, and the Oxo cube was born.

Building on the name: an early advertisement for Fluid Oxo.

RECIPES

BEFORE 1910 was the time of Mrs Beeton when cooking methods were very different from those used today. All chopping, slicing and making purées had to be done by hand – there were no blenders or food processors to make preparation easier.

A cookery book produced by the Liebig Company in 1893 suggested a recipe for Rook Pie, using puff pastry and four rooks! Included here is a latter-day recipe which uses many of the same ingredients, but substitutes pigeons for the rooks.

PARMESAN SOUP

Fresh grated Parmesan cheese is best, but ready-grated is easier and tastes very good.

SERVES 6

1½oz (40g) butter/margarine
1oz (25g) flour
2 red Oxo cubes dissolved in 3pts (1.8 litres) hot water
2 carrots, grated
1 bouquet garni
2 onions, thinly sliced
½ head celery, finely chopped
salt and pepper
3oz (75g) Parmesan cheese, grated
2oz (50g) macaroni (optional)

Melt the butter/margarine in a saucepan, add the flour and stir. Add the stock, carrots, bouquet garni, onions, celery, salt and pepper and bring to the boil. Stir in the cheese, reduce the heat, cover with a lid and simmer for 15–25 minutes or until the vegetables are tender. If using macaroni, cook it in plenty of boiling water for 5 minutes or until tender, drain, and add it to the soup before removing the bouquet garni and serving.

TOMATO PIE

Can be eaten as a supper dish on its own or accompanied by either cold meat or cheese.

SERVES 4

1½lb (675g) tomatoes
1 red Oxo cube
salt and pepper
3oz (75g) fresh breadcrumbs
1oz (25g) butter/margarine

Skin the tomatoes by scalding with boiling water and cut into thick slices. Grease a pie dish with melted butter/margarine and lay in the tomato slices. Crumble the Oxo cube over the tomatoes and season with salt and pepper. Cover with the breadcrumbs and dot the butter/margarine in small lumps over the top. Bake in a hot oven (400°F, 200°C, Gas mark 6) for 20–30 minutes until golden brown.

PIGEON AND RED WINE PIE

The original of this recipe suggested *rooks* – but today pigeons make an excellent substitute.

SERVES 4

2 oven-ready pigeons
8oz (225g) topside beef
4oz (100g) bacon
2 hard boiled eggs (size 2–3)
salt and pepper
¼pt (150ml) dry red wine
1 red Oxo cube dissolved in ½pt (300ml) hot water
1lb (450g) prepared puff pastry
1 egg (size 5), beaten

Split each bird in two. Cut the beef in small thin slices; cut the bacon in strips and slice the eggs. Place the beef, bacon, eggs and pigeon halves in a pie dish and season. Add the wine to the Oxo stock. Pour in sufficient stock to three-quarters fill the pie dish. Cover with puff pastry, make a hole in the centre, glaze with the beaten egg and cook in a hot oven (450°F, 230°C, gas mark 8) until the pastry has risen and set (15–20 minutes) then lower heat to moderate (350°F, 180°C, gas mark 4) and bake for 1½ hours longer, covering the pastry with foil if it is getting too brown. Before serving the pie, fill with the remainder of the reheated Oxo stock, through the centre hole.

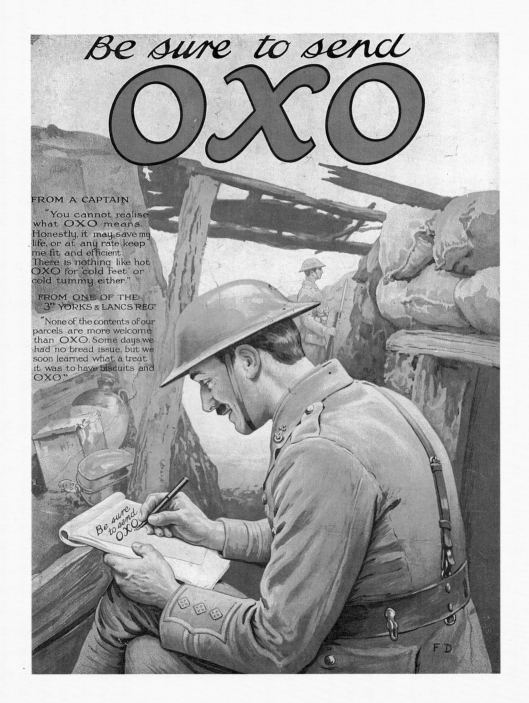

1910~1935

SETTING THE SCENE

THE Oxo cube made its debut in a time of extraordinary change. Advances of every kind were being made with dazzling speed. It was a time of immense excitement and challenge socially and politically.

In 1910 very few people had motor cars; by 1935 there were flights round the world. In 1910 there were radios, though not for general public use, and the cinema was in its silent infancy; by 1935 over three million people had wireless licences and the motion picture industry had achieved enormous and sophisticated success.

A lightning tour through those first twenty-five years of the Oxo cube's existence leaves one amazed at the breadth of progress and discovery. There is also much that is interestingly familiar, with the continuous themes of strikes, unemployment, troubles in Ireland and world conflict. The names change, the news doesn't . . .

1910
George V came to the throne. The first Labour Exchange opened; Crippen was hanged; Thomas Beecham's first opera season began at Covent Garden; and the Girl Guide Movement was founded.

1911
There were suffragette riots in Whitehall; the Commons voted for payment of MPs (£400 per annum) and Alexander's Ragtime Band made its début.

1912
Scott reached the South Pole; the *Titanic* sank; and the statue of Peter Pan went up in Kensington Gardens. Stainless steel was invented; and there came the news that five million Americans went to the cinema every day. London now had 40 cinemas and Charles Pathé had produced the first News Film.

1913
Mrs Pankhurst was sentenced for inciting people to place explosives outside Lloyd George's house; the Women's Franchise Bill was rejected in the Commons; and the first woman magistrate in England, Miss Emily Dawson, was appointed.

1914
War was declared on Germany; £1 and 10 shilling notes were issued.

1915
Albert Einstein published his theory of relativity; the Women's Institute was founded in Britain; and the Germans first used poison gas on the Western Front.

1916
Lloyd George became Prime Minister of a coalition government; the National Savings Movement was founded in Britain and as a result of work on war casualties plastic surgery was developed.

1917
The Russian revolution; the Tsar abdicated. Russia made peace with Germany and the US declared war on Germany.

1918
In Russia, the Tsar and his family were executed. In Britain, food shortages led to the establishment of National Food Kitchens and rationing; and women over 30 got the vote. Traffic lights were installed in New York City. In November the Armistice, which ended the First World War, was signed.

1919
Lady Astor became the first woman MP to take her seat in the House of Commons. Alcock and Brown flew the Atlantic and in July peace was celebrated in Britain. Edwin Lutyens submitted designs for the Cenotaph; Suzanne Lenglen dominated Wimbledon; and Arthur Mee founded his Children's Newspaper.

1920
The League of Nations was founded, but was not supported by the US. In the States, prohibition was declared and Mary Pickford married Douglas Fairbanks.

1921
The BBC was founded; Agatha Christie published her first book (*The Mysterious Affair at Styles*).

1922
The Austin 7 was born; the Tomb of Tutankhamun was discovered. In Britain the coalition government fell; the cocktail was born; and in the General Election Labour achieved second place.

1923
Germany's bank rate was a staggering 90 per cent and the mark dropped to 10,000 million to the pound. Adolf Hitler staged a coup d'état in

Munich (which failed). Sarah Bernhardt died and the Cup Final was played at Wembley for the first time (and won by Bolton Wanderers).

1924

The first Labour Government was formed in Britain; in October the General Election was a resounding victory for the Conservatives; Winston Churchill became Chancellor of the Exchequer. Lenin died; talking pictures were born; and Noel Coward's *The Vortex* was a huge success in the West End of London.

1925

Unemployment Insurance was introduced in Britain; Clarence Birdseye extended his deep-freezing process to pre-cooked food; and people danced the Charleston and read *The Great Gatsby*.

1926

There was a General Strike in Britain; the Electricity Board was established; Rudolph Valentino died; and *Winnie-the-Pooh* was published. Queen Elizabeth II was born.

1927

Mein Kampf (volume two) by Adolf Hitler was published; the German economy collapsed.

1928

Lady Chatterley and Mickey Mouse both first saw the light of day; Hoover was elected President of the US and Chiang Kai-Shek became President of China. Penicillin was discovered by Alexander Fleming and in Britain women over 21 were allowed to vote.

1929

Labour came into power; the US stock market collapsed; the Museum of Modern Art was opened in New York. The first colour film was shown; Ernest Hemingway's *A Farewell to Arms* was published and Graf Zeppelin made numerous successful intercontinental flights.

1930

Mahatma Gandhi began his campaign of Civil Disobedience; the *Daily Worker* was launched, and Don Bradman scored 334 runs for Australia in the Ashes. There were nearly two million telephones and just over three million wireless licences in Great Britain, and Amy Johnson flew solo from London to Australia in 19½ days.

1931

The Delhi pact was made between the Viceroy of India and Gandhi. The British government's economy measures provoked riots in London and Glasgow, and a second National Coalition Government was formed under MacDonald.

1932

Hitler was runner-up in the German presidential elections; and the first Autobahn was opened in Germany. Oswald Mosley founded the British Union of Fascists, Sir Thomas Beecham founded the London Philharmonic Orchestra, and Shirley Temple made her début.

1933

Hitler became the German Chancellor, the persecution of the Jews began in Germany and the Nazi party suppressed all other parties.

1934

Hitler had become Führer and Winston Churchill warned Parliament of the German air menace. Gordonstoun school and the Glyndebourne Festival were both founded; driving tests were introduced in Britain, and there was a regular air mail service from London to Australia.

1935

War began between Italy and Abyssinia; Stanley Baldwin formed a National Government in Britain; and the 30mph speed limit was enforced in certain areas. The 35mm 'Kodachrome' film was devised; and George Gershwin composed *Porgy and Bess*.

It was a brave and amazing new world . . .

REAL LIFE

AWAY from the boundaries of conflict and the corridors of power, there were more immense changes. 1910 was a good time to be rich and a dreadful time to be poor. Great Britain was the largest exporter in the world. Income tax was 1s. 2d. in the pound and a middle class family would have an income of between £700 and £1000 a year; a school teacher and an industrial worker would earn £75 a year and an agricultural worker a maximum of 18 shillings a week. Factory women got about 8 shillings a week.

The rich ate hugely, led by King Edward VII (seven courses was the norm at a dinner party), played games earnestly, fished, shot game and travelled the world, some purely in pursuit of pleasure, others blazing pioneering trails that broadened the Empire and expanded the scope of British business and influence.

Workers' hours were long. For the unemployed there was no 'welfare state' and any relief was small. Although the National Insurance Act in 1911 insured workers for a maximum of 7s. 6d. for the first five weeks only, and the old age pension was 5s. a week paid to the over 70s, Britain was better off than most other countries in the world.

About the time the Cube was born, there was a surge of new industries; rayon dyes, telephone, wireless and photographic apparatus, motor cars and aircraft all had to be manufactured;

and there was a surprising growth in such areas as retailing and advertising. The other unexpected factor in the Edwardian equation was the large number of women working outside the home – 30 per cent of the working population in 1911. And yet they did not have the vote. Suffragettes rioted in Whitehall, chained themselves to railings and went on hunger strike. It was a long battle.

The 1914–18 war did actually mean a higher standard of living for the poor: a soldier wasn't just paid; allowances also went to his family. But standards of housing remained poor.

The Housing Act passed in 1919 allowed councils to build houses for letting; by 1931 one and a half million had gone up. And the suburb was born: leafy utopias for the middle classes,

ABOVE
A newspaper from 14 May, 1926.

BELOW
In 1921 the Taunton car was sold
ready for the road at £550.

Lyons Corner House (for a slap-up luncheon for 1s. 6d.) and the cinema (for an hour or two of steamy romance or side-splitting comedy). There was a cocktail shaker in every well-appointed home, ever more daring books to read and plays to see, and a general feeling that life had become exhilarating, exciting and much more promising in every way.

WOMEN'S LOT

The demand for equal rights was not born with Germaine Greer or even Mrs Pankhurst; it had begun in Victorian times. The cosy vision of women by the hearth rocking cradles was a middle class fantasy; in reality women had been working in factories since the beginning of the industrial revolution, to help feed the many occupants of the cradles.

BELOW
Mrs Pethick Lawrence, editor of the *Votes for Women* newspaper, being arrested in August 1913 after leading a peaceful deputation to Parliament.

who could catch the new underground railway to work.

The Twenties was a schizophrenic era: the age of the cocktail, the Charleston and jazz; of the cinema idol and the bright young things.

There was also massive unemployment and very little unemployment money. The miners were supported in 1926 by the General Council of the TUC in a General Strike; the middle classes organized to break the strike, driving buses and trams, and keeping services going.

On the other hand, life was a lot more fun if you could afford it. There were motor cars; you could play gramophone records, do the Charleston and the Blackbottom in the new Dance Halls, and visit such pleasure palaces as

However, family planning meant smaller families, there were reforms to the divorce laws giving women more rights in the courts, and Edwardian feminists demanded that part of a husband's income should go to his wife as wages.

There was, of course, resistance to all this. Some distinguished scientists proposed that women were less capable than men due to their physiological make-up, and some thought of the suffragettes as crazed and embittered beings.

But during the war women worked, in factories and hospitals and on the land. They helped to win the war, and this indisputably helped to win them the vote. In 1919 the Sex Discrimination Removal Act was passed, allowing women equal rights with men in certain professions. Women were also employed in offices, shops and restaurants. They were confident, independent and determined to remain that way.

Between the two wars, the size of working class families also went down, as Marie Stopes gave her series of lectures on birth control and opened clinics all over the country.

Probably the most exciting time for women in the whole of this century was the Twenties. Freed from the strictures of pre-war morality and conventions, they found themselves reborn socially, sexually and intellectually. Men (particularly of the older generation) watched with horror and alarm as they cut off their hair, revealed their legs, smoked, danced the night away unchaperoned in night clubs, drove motor cars, talked daringly about sex and generally disgraced their forebears. They did, however, go on to marry respectably and to rear families of their own, and in good conditions, too. A middle class lady in the Thirties had an amazingly easy time of it; domestic staff was cheap and quite a modest income would hire a cook, housemaid, a nanny and a gardener, and since most food was delivered to the door, it is hard to imagine how she filled her day.

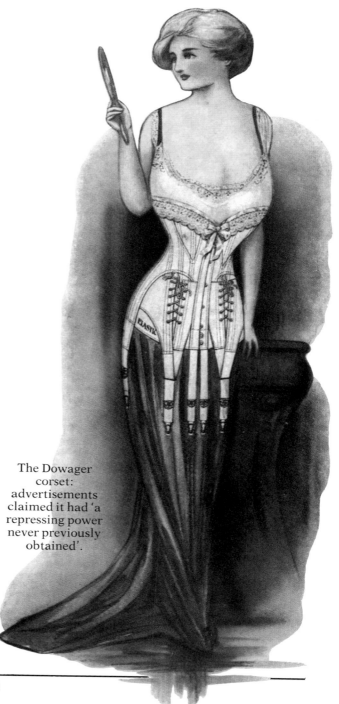

The Dowager corset: advertisements claimed it had 'a repressing power never previously obtained'.

Before the First World War women were still wearing
ankle-length skirts and elaborate hairstyles.

DRESSED FOR IT

The huge change in women's clothes during this twenty-five year period tells more than anything else, perhaps, how their lives changed too.

In 1910 women were still in whalebone corsets from bust to thigh; they wore long skirts and had long, elaborately dressed hair. Laundry all had to be done by hand. During the war women went into trousers, dungarees and overalls; they were hardly likely to climb out of them and back into their restricting clothes. Trousers weren't considered real fashion for a while, but skirts climbed steadily from ankle level in 1918 to knee-high in the late Twenties. The adaptation of the army greatcoat into the trench coat met huge applause, and the trench coat has been with us ever since.

As a result of sugar and butter rationing, cycling, and playing tennis and hockey, many women were much thinner in the Twenties. They looked suddenly boyish, with small bobbed heads on skinny figures and long legs under short skirts. The bob gave way to the shingle and then the bingle (a mixture of both). Smoking in public became acceptable (through ever-longer cigarette holders) and so did lipstick and nail varnish. Sports clothes made their appearance; a pullover and pleated skirt for golf, a cotton

ABOVE
Afternoon dresses of 1927.

RIGHT
Practical fashion: in the Twenties
women's clothes became more
relaxed and hairstyles shorter and
freer.

Cool, calm and collected: the women of the Thirties.

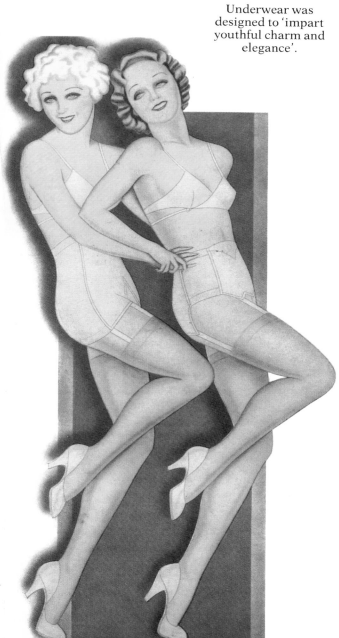

Underwear was designed to 'impart youthful charm and elegance'.

smock and trousers for gardening. The jersey was born and Chanel made it high fashion. Pyjama suits were a craze, with wide flapping trousers, usually made of floppy rayon (the fabric of the Twenties); in the evenings huge ostrich fans and feathers dangled from bare bangled arms. Women flocked to men's shops to buy cardigans, socks, ties and sleeveless v-necked sweaters.

By 1927 skirts had begun to drop again; jackets and hair lengthened, too, and the more languid elegance of the Thirties made its appearance. Evening dresses were longer, with dipping handkerchief hems and daring bare backs. Silky day dresses clung to the newly curving figures. The bathing suit remained hideously restricting in heavy jersey, usually belted (the first two-piece appeared in 1934); the beret became high fashion and so did tweed suits and brogues.

By the mid Thirties the look was more grown up and ladylike to go with the times; the suffragette and the flapper had passed into fancy-dressed history.

The women of the Thirties were cooler, calmer and very sure of who they wanted to be.

ON THE HOME FRONT

Life in the kitchen wasn't a great deal of fun at the time when the cube entered it. It revolved around the range, a huge, temperamental monster requiring constant feeding, cleaning and black-leading. On a good day, if you were lucky, the monster would cook, heat water and warm the kitchen (which was of doubtful value in summer). Mrs Beeton's admonition that the successful housewife must, above all, be an early riser was probably as much in deference to the stove as anything else. Even if the successful housewife wasn't going to light the thing, clean its flues and load it with coal, the maidservant responsible would certainly need supervision.

Apart from the range, cleaning the kitchen was hard work. There were no wipe-clean surfaces; just wood which had to be scrubbed daily. The floor was either red-tiled or, in more up-to-date establishments, covered in linoleum, which had to be scrubbed, too, with shredded soap. Squeezy mops and detergents would have seemed dazzlingly modern and labour-saving!

Refrigerators belonged in science fiction; if ice was required for a dinner party, it had to be bought, wrapped in an old flannel and buried in the ground until required. Laundry was a hugely time-consuming, back-breaking job, taking at least one whole day a week. The washing was boiled in a copper, scrubbed, wrung (probably in one of the new-fangled wringers) and dried, then ironed by flat irons heated on the range.

Cooking was a haphazard occupation; there were no settings on the ovens so temperatures were mostly confined to hot or very hot and a lot of guesswork was done. If a recipe asked for a cool oven, the cook was advised to leave the door open. Hygiene was not of a high standard, and of course there were no convenience foods – with the exception of the Cube. The larder was still a necessity for storing food, but with the increasing efficiency of the local grocer and his ever-increasing stock, food supplies could at least be replenished more frequently and easily. Nevertheless, the kitchen wasn't really a place in which to cook, and certainly not to enjoy life; it was a prison where women were sentenced to hard labour.

Gradually things got better. Gas ovens made an appearance shortly after 1910 (although they still had their drawbacks, being difficult to light and with burners and pipes that were constantly

The kitchen range: a huge, temperamental monster requiring constant attention.

clogged). And as electricity became more and more common in homes, so kitchens became cleaner.

Changes were not drastic until well into the Twenties. While the First World War was being fought, nobody had much time or attention to spare for the housewife. But in 1926, the Central Electricity Board was created by Act of Parliament, which initiated the building of the 'grid' – high-voltage transmission lines which carried electricity right across the country and into virtually every home. This transformed kitchen life, and that of its main occupants, women. Gradually such wonders as refrigerators and electric lights found their way into most homes. For the first time ordinary women were able to enjoy the time they spent in their kitchens.

ENTER THE CUBE

IT is intriguing to see how the Oxo cube fits so neatly into this multi-coloured background of discovery and change – how it went out into the world in its dashing red and white packaging and did something for everybody.

It brought nourishment to the poor, comfort in the trenches, sustenance to explorers, and (as one of the first convenience foods) was an invaluable aid to the cooks of the world.

Until there was Oxo, stock and gravy were made by boiling bones and stripping carcasses. To be able to replace this by adding the Cube to a cup of hot water meant hours of time and work saved, and an arguably much better taste too. Oxo, with the vacuum cleaner, electric light and detergent, has become something we take utterly for granted, and without which we would find ourselves firmly back into the hard labour league.

From Day One, the Oxo cube's image has been irresistibly cheerful, linked not only with such physical comfort as warmth and flavour, but (by way of brilliantly up-beat promotion) smiling children and good-natured adults, charming packaging and wantable offers. You do not necessarily smile when you think of flour or sugar or even ice cream; but Oxo's associations are entirely happy. No wonder it was so welcome in the trenches and so obligatory on expeditions. It meant home warmth, and a feeling that everything was going to be all right in the end.

The Cube was launched (again predictably ahead of its time) simply by a direct selling operation. Leaflets were pushed under doors telling grateful members of the public that if they went to their nearest neighbourhood grocery store, they could buy the hitherto expensive Oxo fluid in cheap and wonderfully convenient cubes, for sale in tins of 6, 12, 50 or 100.

Oxo cubed: the Extract in a more convenient and its most famous form.

Packed in Tins of
6 cubes: 12 cubes:
50 cubes: 100 cubes.

Oxo Cubes
are the greatest advance in food invention since men began to eat and women learned to cook

cup of Oxo would not only revive and warm them, but also make them ready for their next Oxo-based meal. Each dish had Oxo in its name as well as amongst its ingredients, and managed to use a lot of cubes. Today not many recipes recommend two cubes per dish, but in 1915 even something as simple as curried eggs for four demanded two.

LEFT
The professional touch: the original Oxo salesmen's brochure.

BELOW
Oxo with everything: one of the early Oxo cookbooks.

The launch was a wild success. People flocked to the grocery shops and bought cubes in thousands. Interestingly, it didn't affect sales of Oxo fluid initially as that was bought by the better off. It was the poor who took the Cube to their hearts and their stomachs, making literally a meal of it, alongside a hunk of bread at the end of a bad week. The Company had already learnt the value of promoting their product via cookery books; and in 1911 and 1915, charming new Oxo cookery books appeared, containing many assurances about the delicious and revitalizing properties of Oxo, and recipes. They also promoted a kind of perpetual motion for the Cube, assuring readers that in times of weariness a hot

WARM COMFORT

Oxo began to travel the world in all directions. In 1911 Captain Scott went to the South Pole and gave Oxo the highest possible accolade by taking it with him. He wrote and said how useful it had been and enclosed photographs of his expedition members actually having an Oxo drink. *The Sketch* magazine published a wonderfully graphic advertisement at the time showing a polar bear in the howling wilderness snuffling at a jar of Oxo. Unfortunately it was soon discovered that no polar bears exist in the Antarctic so the Company had to quickly change the advertisement to feature penguins instead.

ABOVE
Cold comfort: Oxo goes to the Antarctic with Scott.

BELOW LEFT AND RIGHT
When it was discovered that there are no polar bears there, the advertisement was changed to show penguins instead.

In 1919 the Cube flew the Atlantic with Alcock and Brown – a glowing testimonial from Sir John Alcock spoke of how it had sustained them during their sixteen-hour journey. But its proudest time during the early days was during the First World War when it went to the trenches in literally thousands of tins. The Cube was in the standard set of emergency rations for the troops alongside a tin of Fray Bentos corned beef, if they were lucky. There are several stories on record of the tins of Oxo or corned beef literally saving men's lives; being in their emergency packs, they deflected bullets and pieces of shrapnel with surprising efficiency.

One of the first offers associated with Oxo was for the Oxo Trench Heater; you could send out to your Man in the Trenches a set of 6 Oxo cubes, 6 lighters and a collapsible stand to support his mess tin. In the misery and mire of the trenches, where lighting a fire was impossible and warmth so desperately needed, the heaters must have seemed magical devices.

ABOVE
Flying high with Oxo: Alcock and Brown took the Cube from London to Australia on their inaugural flight.

RIGHT
In (almost) every soldier's kitbag: the Oxo Trench Heater, warming the army's hearts and stomachs in the First World War.

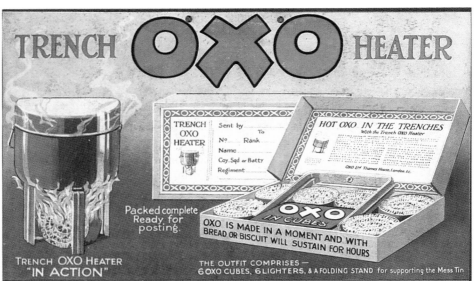

TRENCH OXO HEATER

TRENCH OXO HEATER

HOT OXO IN THE TRENCHES
With the Trench OXO Heater

OXO Ltd Thames House, London, E.C.

OXO CUBES

OXO IS MADE IN A MOMENT AND WITH BREAD OR BISCUIT WILL SUSTAIN FOR HOURS

Packed complete Ready for posting.

TRENCH OXO HEATER "IN ACTION"

THE OUTFIT COMPRISES —
6 OXO CUBES, 6 LIGHTERS, & A FOLDING STAND for supporting the Mess Tin

Telling and selling: early Oxo advertisements.

PREJUDICE AND PRIDE

Just before the war the Company suffered from some unpleasant prejudice. Anti-German feeling was high and anybody or thing that seemed even remotely connected with Germany had a hard time. The German pork butchers, who were in nearly every town, were vandalized, and so were the pastry shops; Liebig, of the Liebig Extract of Meat Company which manufactured the Oxo cube, was instantly recognizable as a German name, which lent undesirable associations to the company.

The notion of making Lord Hawke the new chairman of Oxo was a brilliant one. Lord Hawke was a major shareholder, one of the great cricketers of his day, President of the MCC and something of a national hero. He took his place at the head of the Company with pride and pleasure, adding aristocratic associations to those of physical prowess, fitness and athletic achievement that Oxo already possessed to a large degree, and bestowing upon the Company a symbol of all that was best in traditional British life.

WAR AND PEACE

The Company had a superb war record; it met every demand and fulfilled every order, despite loss of ships and staff and having to train inexperienced girls in the factories. It delivered 100 million Oxo cubes and twice that number of cans of corned beef during the four years, and must have helped to win the war.

In other ways, too, the Company was a benign force; it set up a Benevolent Fund for employees and a convalescent home for factory workers. Handbills produced during the war were intensely patriotic: 'Oxo Cubes are British', they said. 'They are made in Britain by a British company with British labour.'

The Company was now housed in a superb building near Southwark Bridge. Built in 1912, Thames House could justifiably be called an architectural treasure. Everything seemed to conspire to make Oxo a national institution.

And indeed this is what it went on to be. Very soon after the war, Oxo became not just a food and part of the fabric of kitchen and family life,

LEFT
National hero: Lord Hawke became Chairman in 1913.

RIGHT
Benign force: the women employees of Oxo Ltd doing their bit on Empire Flag Day.

LEFT
Oxo is British: this Empire Flag Day signboard left that in no doubt.

BELOW
Health assured: Oxo health insurance, offered free in 1921. The scheme was so over-subscribed that eventually it had to be abandoned.

but also a byword for health and health care, fitness and a still more basic security in life insurance. In 1921 Oxo offered everybody between the ages of fourteen and sixty a free gift of twelve weeks' health insurance. The premium was provided by proof of weekly purchases of Oxo; by spending a shilling and upwards a week on Oxo, you could insure yourself for benefits up to £7 10s, covering seventeen specific common illnesses. In the absence of a state health service it was a stroke of genius. Nothing could have given the company more integrity or made it seem more substantial. In fact it was too successful; so many applications flooded in that eventually the scheme had to be abandoned.

GIVING THINGS AWAY

Oxo also became a byword during this period for gifts – or near-gifts. In 1923 they gave away 50,000 Christmas stockings to 'Oxo children'. In order to get one, the Oxo child's parents had to save up 120 cube wrappers. All the stockings were claimed and six million cubes sold in the process.

In 1925 Little Miss Betty Oxo was born; nearly 17 inches high, with a 'beautifully modelled and expressive face, jointed arms and legs, and smart fashionable clothes'. The doll was a wild success.

Then there was the Oxo book of nursery rhymes, the Oxo painting books and *The Oxo Book of Magic* (written by Uncle Magicus, the children's friend). And immortalized for ever was the red Oxo van, scaled down to Dinky Toy size and sold for 3d. One of them fetched £550 at Sotheby's recently, more than the real van had cost when it first went on the road.

NATIONAL SERVICE

Oxo did a lot for the nation in a modest way. In the first place it tirelessly promoted the notion of physical fitness and care. There was the annual London to Brighton walk under Oxo's sponsorship, and Oxo Handbooks for Nurses. In 1930 Sir William Arbuthnot Lane, president of the New Health Society, visited Oxo's factory and was photographed looking stern but pleased with his cup of Oxo; and of course Lord Hawke, with his title and county cricket connections, continued

ABOVE
Sir William Arbuthnot Lane visiting the Oxo factory.

BELOW
The Oxo stand at the 1924 British Empire Exhibition.

to bring to the company an aura of association with the landed gentry and the spirit that built the British Empire.

At every sporting event Oxo was there, with cups of hot Oxo for athletes, cyclists and footballers, and a high degree of visibility of its product for the spectators. Oxo figured in the diets of winning teams and champions, and in 1921 an Oxo sports ground was opened in Bromley.

Three Oxo challenge trophies, presented at the Royal Agricultural Society each year for the best Hereford, Sussex and Aberdeen Angus bulls, made a marvellous link with country and agricultural life, with wholesome and healthful associations. In 1924, the Duke of York (later

ABOVE
Feeling bullish: the Oxo challenge trophy for the best
Sussex bull, presented annually.
BELOW
Royal approval: the Duke of York (later King George VI)
on a working visit to the Oxo factory in 1924.

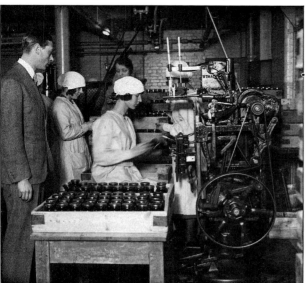

King George VI) not only visited the Oxo factory, but also operated the machine which chopped the solid extract into cubes and wrapped them up. There were several references to Oxo as a harbinger of comfort and joy in a stirring piece of popular literature published in *The People* in 1930; *Not So Quiet* by Helen Zenna Smith, 'a human moving narrative (frank at times)' about women's role in the Great War, when alongside driving ambulances and cleaning war vehicles, the women made, drank and clearly drew comfort from a lot of cups of Oxo.

Oxo had become most truly a part of British national life.

VARIATION ON A THEME

In the early Thirties the Oxo company launched several new products, all in tablet form. There was Oxade Cocoa, Oxade Lemonade and Orangeade, and even a revival of beef tea, named Bifti. There were also table jellies and Oxo toffees. None were successful. So totally had Oxo established itself as being synonymous with beef that it was not easy for it suddenly to become synonymous with oranges and lemons. But it all probably served to push the Oxo name and message nearer the heart of every home.

Until 1921, every single cube had been wrapped by hand; a formidable achievement considering the 100 million cubes that had been wrapped during the war. But in 1921, a new machine that wrapped the cubes was installed, hugely increasing productivity.

In 1929 a new formula was launched. It was more easily soluble, and the cubes were bigger. This meant changing everything: machinery, wrapping, packing, cartons. It was worth it; the housewife took the new, bigger and better cube to her larder with more enthusiasm than ever.

OXO & SODA

SOLD HERE

INVIGORATES · A COOLING & STRENGTHENING DRINK · SUSTAINS

OXO LIMITED. LONDON

LEFT AND BELOW Variations on a theme: the Oxo name on new products.

OPPOSITE PAGE, LEFT Fighting fit: Oxo goes to war and improves the military health.

OPPOSITE PAGE, RIGHT Oxo is beautiful – or how Oxo came out of the kitchen and into the boudoir.

OXO CHOCOLATE 1D.

REJECTED COINS

Delicious and Sustaining

TELLING AND SELLING

Oxo advertising has always been genuinely innovative, approaching the media and the message in highly ingenious and original ways.

A stirring campaign from the Front in 1915 showed a heavily bandaged soldier lying in bed, a pot of Oxo at his side to aid his recovery and (perhaps rather less ideally) a cigarette in his hand. The picture was taken by a hospital orderly, who assured the reader that Oxo had been invaluable in the soldier's recovery. Another testimonial-based advertisement, reproducing letters from 'a 2nd Lieutenant', 'One of

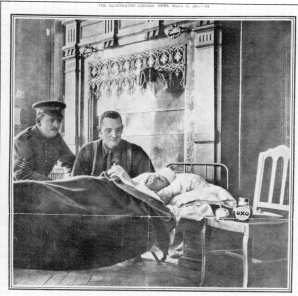

OXO IN EMERGENCIES.

This interesting photograph and letter have been sent to OXO Ltd. from one of the British Hospitals in France.

A village at the Front, NORTH FRANCE.

"I enclose photo taken at a field hospital at present situated in an old French chateau, a few miles from the firing line, where only the worst cases that cannot travel are kept.

It did not strike me that this would make a good advertisement for your firm until after it was developed. I took it as I wanted a record of one of the most interesting cases it has been my privilege to tend. He was badly wounded in five places by shrapnel bullets—one through his palate—another through his forearm, a fourth and fifth in his back. It is a remarkable case, but with the careful treatment and constant care that have been his lot, he has recovered, as you see by the photo.

Owing to his palate being broken, he could only take liquid food, and I have no hesitation in saying that we have found OXO to be invaluable in keeping up his strength, and he prefers it to any other food."

OXO IS INVALUABLE IN THE HOSPITALS AS WELL AS IN THE TRENCHES.

OXO Ltd., Thames House, London, E.C.

The beauty of health

When you take Oxo regularly you are using its rich beef-nourishment to maintain your physical resources in the glowing vigour of buoyant vitality

OXO

OXO Limited – Thames House – London, E·C·4

the Royal Scots' and 'From a Soldier's Mother', had the same persuasively real-life quality.

After the War, Oxo entered the nursery as well as the kitchen, and also the boudoir. A slightly mysterious, haunting beauty looks confidently out from the page, above the caption 'The Beauty of Health' and copy extolling the 'glowing vigour of buoyant vitality'. Rosy-cheeked children with curls and smiles vouch more persuasively and engagingly for Oxo's body-building properties. In 1922 the marvellous 'Mighty Atom' campaign was launched – a wonderful representation of a

giant Oxo cube beaming out goodness (with a herd of cattle thrown in for good measure). It used the highly economic style of copywriting, all short sentences and vivid imagery, that is still fashionable now.

The Oxo Habit, the Oxo Nightcap and the Cook's Best Friend have all passed into the vernacular; but perhaps most famous of all is the Oxo Tower. This went up in 1930 at Blackfriars, beaming out the Logo perpetually to anyone who looked across the Thames from north to south,

Mother's help: Oxo was sold as an essential ingredient in a healthy child's diet.

52

Powerful advertising:
the Mighty Atom
campaign was
launched in 1922.

ABOVE
The Oxo Tower, built in Blackfriars, London in 1930 and an architectural curiosity ever since.

LEFT AND BELOW
By the end of the Oxo Company's first twenty-five years its advertising had helped to establish it in the nation's hearts.

and hugely praised as the culmination of the first twenty-five years of outstanding advertising that the company had accomplished.

'The proprietors of Oxo,' wrote a reporter in the *World's Press News* in 1933, 'have won a high reputation for enterprise in the matter of advertising; perhaps one of their most striking achievements was the construction of the tower of their Blackfriars warehouse, in such a way that the windows spell Oxo. The effect is to make the Oxo message the most prominent advertising feature in the district.' It was a fine and fitting finale to the first twenty-five years.

RECIPES

THE introduction in 1910 of the Oxo cube – ready-made stock in a little hot water – must have been a boon, helping cooks to become more adventurous with their recipes. Kitchen life was beginning to change and more recipe books were becoming available. House-wives were encouraged to try out new ideas and tastes – like apple soup and iced bouillon – though recipes were not so expertly put together as they are in cookery books today. Here are updated versions of some of the recipes being produced by Oxo during this time.

BEEF OLIVES

One of the tastiest beef dishes – an ideal dinner party recipe for a cool evening with hungry friends.

SERVES 4

3oz (75g) parsley and thyme stuffing mix
4 × 4oz (100g) slices of topside of beef, beaten flat
1 tbs oil
1 medium onion, peeled and sliced
1 tbs flour
1 red Oxo cube dissolved in ½pt (300ml) hot water
1 tsp Worcestershire sauce
4 tbs tomato ketchup
salt and pepper

Make the stuffing; divide and spread over the slices of meat. Roll them up and tie with fine string. Heat the oil and fry the olives until brown all over. Remove them and place in an oven-proof casserole. Add the onion to the oil and fry until brown. Stir in the flour and cook for one minute. Add the Oxo stock, Worcestershire sauce, ketchup, salt and pepper and bring to the boil, stirring. Pour the sauce over the olives, cover and cook in a moderate oven (350°F, 180°C, gas mark 4) for 1 to 1¼ hrs or until tender. Remove the string before serving.

KIDNEY OMELETTES

This is a savoury way of using up left-over kidneys from the freezer.

SERVES 2

2oz (50g) butter/margarine
2 lambs kidneys, skinned, cored and chopped
1 red Oxo cube
4 eggs (size 3 or 4), separated
1 tsp parsley, chopped
salt and pepper

Melt 1oz (25g) butter/margarine in a pan, add kidneys and sauté for about 2 minutes. Crumble in the Oxo cube. Beat up the egg yolks with parsley, salt and pepper. Whip the egg whites until stiff, and fold into the yolks. Stir in the kidneys very gently. Divide the whole mixture in half. Melt ½oz (12g) butter/margarine in a small frying pan, pour in half the mixture and cook gently until set. Fold over and serve very hot. Repeat for the second omelette.

ENDIVE AND EGGS

This unusual and tasty combination makes an ideal light supper or lunch dish.

SERVES 4

1 large white endive (chicory)
1 red Oxo cube dissolved in ½pt (300ml) hot water
1 tsp tomato ketchup
salt and pepper
1oz (25g) butter/margarine
4 eggs (size 3 or 4)
4 slices of bread, toasted

Peel and wash the endive; pour boiling water over to remove bitter taste, then plunge into cold water for 10 minutes. Drain, squeeze dry and chop finely. Place the endive in a saucepan, add the Oxo stock, tomato ketchup, salt and pepper. Bring to the boil and simmer until tender. Drain and stir in the butter/margarine. Poach the eggs, and toast the bread. Divide the endive between four slices of toast and place a poached egg on top of each. Serve hot.

VEGETABLE HOTCH POTCH

An inexpensive and satisfying meatless dish.

SERVES 4–6

2lb (900g) potatoes, peeled and sliced
1lb (450g) onions, peeled and sliced
4oz (100g) mushrooms, sliced
1½oz (40g) sago
salt and pepper
4 red Oxo cubes dissolved in 2 pts (1.2 litres) hot water

Arrange the potatoes and onions in separate layers in a casserole, with mushrooms, a sprinkling of sago, pepper and a little salt between each layer, finishing with a layer of potatoes on top. Cover with the Oxo stock and bake at 325°F, 160°C, gas mark 3 for about 2 hours.

ORANGE GRAVY

This is delicious with duck, goose, pork or gammon.

SERVES 4

rind of small orange, finely pared
½ tsp sugar
1 red Oxo cube dissolved in ½pt (300ml) hot water
½ tsp arrowroot
1 wineglassful port wine
cayenne pepper

Add the orange rind and sugar to the Oxo stock, bring to the boil and simmer for 5 minutes. Blend the arrowroot and port together and add to the stock. Stir in a dash of Cayenne pepper and boil until slightly thickened. Strain the gravy and serve it very hot.

CORNED BEEF HASH

This excellent family dish originated in America.

SERVES 4

2oz (50g) butter/margarine
1 medium onion, finely chopped
1 medium green pepper, finely chopped
12oz (340g) can corned beef, diced small
2lb (900g) potatoes, peeled, boiled and mashed
pinch of pepper
1 red Oxo cube dissolved in ½pt (300ml) of hot milk
4 eggs (size 2 or 3), poached
parsley for garnish

Melt the butter/margarine and gently cook the onion and pepper for about 5 minutes until light brown. Mix corned beef, potatoes, onion and green pepper well together. Add the pepper and Oxo stock. Lightly grease a frying pan and cook hash until brown. Turn on to a hot dish and garnish with the poached eggs and parsley.

CREOLE SAUCE

This goes well with fish dishes or omelettes.

SERVES 4

4oz (100g) butter
2oz (50g) flour
2 red Oxo cubes dissolved in 1pt (600ml) hot water
pinch of salt and pepper
1 small onion, peeled and chopped
1 small green pepper, de-seeded and finely chopped
2 ripe tomatoes, skinned and chopped
2oz (50g) mushrooms, sliced
6 stoned green olives, chopped

Melt 2oz (50g) of the butter/margarine, add flour and stir over a gentle heat until blended and smooth. Add Oxo stock gradually and cook until sauce is thick and smooth. Season. Melt remaining butter/margarine and cook the onion and pepper until lightly browned (about 5 minutes). Add the tomatoes, mushrooms and olives. Cook for 2 minutes then add to the brown sauce. Bring to the boil, check the seasoning and serve hot.

ICED OXO BOUILLON

Ideal for a hot summer day or as an easy starter.

SERVES 2

1 red Oxo cube dissolved in ½pt (300ml) boiling water
2 slices lemon
4 slices cucumber

Pour the Oxo stock into 2 cups or small bowls. Float a slice of lemon and a slice of cucumber on each. Cool and chill in the refrigerator. To serve, replace the cucumber slices with fresh ones and, if desired, add a small lump of ice, crushed.

ONION BUTTER SAUCE

Serve this with steak, liver or burgers.

SERVES 2

3oz (75g) butter/margarine
3oz (75g) onions, chopped very finely
1 red Oxo cube dissolved in ¼pt (150ml) boiling water
1 tbs parsley, chopped
1 tsp Worcestershire sauce

Melt the butter, add the onion and brown slowly for about 10 minutes. Add Oxo stock, parsley and Worcestershire sauce and stir well.

AUBERGINE AU GRATIN

This is a tasty main dish on its own or can be served in smaller portions as a starter.

SERVES 4 (main course)
or 8–10 (starter)

1 large aubergine, peeled and cut into dice
flour for dusting
3 tbs corn oil
2oz (50g) butter/margarine
1oz (25g) flour
1 red Oxo cube dissolved in ½pt (300ml) hot water
½ tsp salt
pinch of pepper
1 tbs tomato purée
6oz (175g) cheddar cheese, grated
2 tbs buttered crumbs

Toss the diced aubergine in the flour until coated lightly all over and sauté in hot oil until golden brown (about 10 minutes). Make a sauce by melting the butter/margarine in a saucepan and stir-ring in the flour over gentle heat. Gradually add the Oxo stock and bring to the boil. Add salt, pepper and tomato purée. Fill a baking dish with alternate layers of aubergine, sauce and cheese. Sprinkle with the buttered crumbs and bake in a moderate oven (375°F, 190°C, gas mark 5) for 25 minutes.

OXO SPREAD

This gives a savoury taste to baked potatoes, plain biscuits etc.

1 red Oxo cube
4oz (100g) butter/margarine

Crumble the Oxo cube into the softened butter/margarine and beat until creamy. Use for sandwiches, snacks and savoury dishes.

WALNUT BITLETS

A quick cocktail snack.

lemon juice
paprika pepper
salt
Oxo spread
40 large shelled walnut halves

Add lemon juice, paprika pepper and salt to taste to a quantity of Oxo Spread (see above). Spread this filling between the walnut halves and sandwich together. Serve as an appetizing savoury for drink and buffet parties.

APPLE SOUP

An absolutely delicious soup which can be served hot or cold.

SERVES 4

1lb (450g) cooking apples, sliced thinly
½ tsp ground ginger
4 cloves
½ tsp curry powder
salt and pepper
2 red Oxo cubes dissolved in 2pts (1.2 litres) hot water
1oz (25g) butter/margarine
1oz (25g) flour

Add the apples and spices to the Oxo stock. Bring to the boil and simmer gently to a pulp. Pass through a sieve or liquidiser, and return to the saucepan. Blend the butter/margarine and flour together, add to the apple pulp, bring to the boil and stir until thickened.

DEVILLED BANANAS

These make an unusual accompaniment to cold cuts of meat.

SERVES 4

1oz (25g) butter/margarine
1oz (25g) red pepper, chopped
1 red Oxo cube
¼ tsp salt
2 tsp chutney, chopped
1 tsp Worcestershire sauce
4 bananas, peeled and cut into 4 portions each

Melt the butter/margarine in a large frying pan. Add red pepper, crumbled Oxo cube, salt, chutney and Worcestershire sauce. Add bananas and gently stir-fry for about 5 minutes. Serve hot.

OXO PARSNIPS

So good they can be eaten on their own or with hot or cold meat dishes, especially pork and bacon.

SERVES 4

1lb (450g) parsnips, peeled and diced
2oz (50g) breadcrumbs
1 red Oxo cube, crumbled
1 egg, (size 3 or 4) beaten
oil for frying

Cook parsnips in boiling water until tender, drain and mash. Mix breadcrumbs and Oxo and add to the mashed parsnips. Bind with the beaten egg, roll into 8 balls, and fry in hot fat.

OXO BISCUITS

A tasty party snack.

3 tbs double cream
2 oz (60g) cream cheese
1 red Oxo cube, crumbled
3 blades of chives, chopped
1 stick celery, finely chopped
1 packet cheese biscuits
Paprika pepper

Beat the cream and cheese together until well blended. Add the Oxo, chives and celery and mix well. Spread the mixture on the biscuits and sprinkle with Paprika pepper; or use to sandwich the biscuits in pairs.

1936~1960

FORWARD TO VICTORY

THE years between 1936 and 1960 were both the darkest and the proudest in Britain's history, and a time of astonishing advance as well. The Second World War was battled through and won; the British people lived to see victory, freedom and undreamed-of prosperity.

During this quarter-century the atom was split and missiles were sent to the moon, many diseases were conquered and people continued to persecute their fellows. The news looked at in retrospect seems repetitive: wars, riots and oppression go hand in hand with increased tolerance, humanity and justice.

Travel shrank the globe; the media expanded knowledge and awareness of every area of existence, and everybody was demanding and expecting more of everything – work, leisure and the general fabric of life.

1936
George V died and Edward VIII succeeded to the throne in January; Baldwin warned Edward VIII that gossip about him and Mrs Simpson was undermining respect for the throne. Mosley led an anti-Jewish march down the Mile End Road. The BBC began sending television signals from Alexandra Palace. In December, Edward VIII abdicated and George VI succeeded to the throne. Shirley Temple signed a five-year film contract for £1,000 per week.

1937
Mussolini visited Berlin; Italy joined Germany and Japan in the Anti-Comintern pact; and under the new Irish Constitution, the Irish Free State became Eire. The first Butlin Holiday camp was opened at Skegness; insulin was first successfully used to treat cases of diabetes; and nylon stockings saw the light of day.

1938
Adolf Hitler became War Minister and Germany annexed Austria. The British Ministry of Labour recommended a week's holiday with pay; *Picture Post* was founded; and *Snow White and the Seven Dwarfs* was packing the cinemas.

1939
The clouds of war were gathering: Chamberlain warned Hitler that he would stand by Poland; women and children were evacuated from London in August; in September Germany invaded Poland and war was declared. All men between 18 and 41 were called up. Polythene was invented; Pan-American Airways began regular commercial flights between the US and Europe; and *Gone with the Wind* was released.

1940
Chamberlain resigned and Churchill formed a coalition government. Italy declared war on France and Britain, and the Battle of Britain reached its peak. In August the Blitz began. The Home Guard was formed, food rationing began; purchase tax was first imposed; and penicillin was developed as an antibiotic.

1941
Rommel crossed into North Africa; Germany invaded Russia; Churchill and Roosevelt signed the Atlantic Charter and the Japanese bombed Pearl Harbor. Double Summer Time was introduced and so was clothes rationing. Terylene was invented; and single women aged 20–30 were declared liable for military service.

1942
Churchill and Stalin met in Moscow; the Allies under Eisenhower landed in North Africa. The atom was split; the Beveridge report on social security was published; and ITMA became a national institution on the radio.

1943
Rommel went into retreat, Mussolini fell, and Churchill, Roosevelt and Stalin met in Teheran. *Oklahoma!* reached the London stage and Frank Sinatra became a pop idol.

Winston Churchill.

1944

The Allies invaded and occupied Italy; the D-Day landing in Normandy was successfully accomplished, and de Gaulle entered Paris. Pay-as-you-earn income tax was introduced; some miners went on strike; and Olivier's *Henry V* was released.

1945

Hitler and Mussolini were both dead: VE day in May marked the end of the war in Europe. In August the first atomic bomb was dropped on Hiroshima and Japan surrendered; and the Nuremberg Trials began in November. De Gaulle became President of France; and in the British general election Labour won a landslide victory. *Animal Farm* and *Brideshead Revisited* were published, and Bebop dancing swept the US.

1946

The United Nations General Assembly held its first session. The Bank of England was nationalized, and the National Health and National Insurance Acts came into force. The Third Programme was inaugurated, and *The Winslow Boy* was on in the West End.

1947

The Independence of India was proclaimed; the first supersonic air flight took place; and the Dead Sea Scrolls were discovered. Coal was nationalized; Princess Elizabeth married Prince Philip; and the big theatre news was *A Street Car named Desire*.

1948

Gandhi was assassinated; the Jewish Provisional Government was formed in Israel; and the People's Republic was formed in Northern China. Bread rationing ended in Britain; the long-playing record and the transistor were both invented; and Prince Charles was born.

1949

Britain recognized the Republic of Ireland as independent, but re-affirmed position of Northern Ireland within the UK. The North Atlantic Treaty was signed; the state of Vietnam was established; and an Apartheid programme began in South Africa. The capital of Israel was moved from Tel Aviv to Jerusalem. There was a dock strike, and George Orwell's *1984* was published.

1950

The USSR and China signed a thirty-year treaty in Moscow. The Korean War began; and Britain recognized the State of Israel. 32,516 people were divorced (as opposed to 8,396 in 1940) and *Call Me Madam* was on the London stage.

1951

Aneurin Bevan and Harold Wilson resigned from the Labour cabinet in protest at the imposition of health service charges; the spies Burgess and Maclean fled to Russia. The Conservatives came back into power; the Festival of Britain drew the world to London; the X-certificate was introduced; and *The Archers* came on the air.

1952

Britain's first atomic bomb tests took place in Australia. A contraceptive tablet was developed. King Farouk abdicated in Egypt; and a state of emergency was declared in Kenya over the Mau Mau disturbances. George VI died and Elizabeth II became queen. Epstein's *Madonna and Child* was unveiled.

1953

Stalin died; Eisenhower was inaugurated president of the US; and Jomo Kenyatta was convicted of managing the Mau Mau in Kenya. Hilary and Tenzing from John Hunt's expedition conquered Everest; Queen Elizabeth II was crowned; and Benjamin Britten composed *Gloriana*. Myxomatosis killed millions of rabbits in Britain and all over Europe. *Roman Holiday* together with the first ever film in Cinemascope, *The Robe*, were the films to see.

1954
Nasser seized power in Egypt, and British troops were evacuated from the Suez Canal. For the first time a connection was proposed between smoking and lung cancer. Billy Graham reached London; and Roger Bannister ran a mile in under four minutes.

1955
Churchill resigned, and was succeeded by Anthony Eden. Britain and the US signed an atomic energy agreement; and border raids between Israel and Jordan increased in intensity. Ruth Ellis was the last woman to be hanged; the Salk vaccine against polio was developed; and commercial TV was launched in Britain.

1956
Bulganin proposed a twenty-year pact of friendship between Russia and the US. The troubles in Cyprus began; and Nasser seized the Suez Canal. The first Aldermaston march by the CND took place and Prince Rainier of Monaco married the American film star Grace Kelly.

1957
Anthony Eden resigned, and Macmillan became Premier. The Rome Treaty establishing the Common Market was signed; and *Sputnik* was launched into space by the Russians. ERNIE drew the first premium bond prizes in Britain; and *My Fair Lady* was the big stage hit.

1958
There were race riots in Nottingham and Notting Hill. The first parking meters were introduced in London, and the last débutantes were presented at court.

1959
Fidel Castro rose to power in Cuba; and the first meeting of the European Court of Human Rights took place. A US aircraft was 'buzzed' in the Berlin air corridor by USSR jet fighters, and the space race continued. The first section of the M1 was opened; the Mini car arrived; and the first Hovercraft crossed the Channel, in two hours. The United Nations condemned apartheid; the Conservatives retained power in Britain; and *Face to Face* broke new ground in television journalism.

1960
Macmillan made his 'Wind of Change' speech. Nixon and John F Kennedy confronted one another on TV; and a state of emergency was proclaimed in Sharpeville, South Africa, after the shooting of 67 black protesters against the Apartheid laws. The Civil Rights Bill was passed in the US, and Mrs Bandaranaike became premier of Ceylon. The Pacemaker device for hearts was developed by surgeons at Birmingham, Princess Margaret married Anthony Armstrong-Jones, and *Saturday Night, Sunday Morning* shook cinema audiences to the core.

The Swinging Sixties had begun . . .

A NEW ERA

ANYONE stepping straight from 1936 to 1960 could well have believed they had arrived on a different planet, not just in a different quarter century. In the Sixties Britain found herself on the threshold of a new social condition altogether, with cars, televisions, well-stocked larders and wardrobes in an enormous proportion of homes and almost full employment. The climate was right for flair, originality and opportunism to prosper. It was a brave new world and the courageous had taken hold of it. But it had been a hard fight . . .

In 1936 the average income was £3 a week. You would then pay between ten and fifteen shillings in rent; you'd need about one shilling a week for clothes, and sixpence for fuel. A newspaper cost one penny, a wireless set about £8 and a 12-oz bar of chocolate one shilling. The really poor lived on

On the airwaves: a 1935 radio advertisement.

a diet consisting mainly of bread, tea and potatoes, and children still frequently suffered from malnutrition. Nobody realized what a health hazard smoking was, it was a cheap pleasure at sixpence for fifteen, hugely glamorized by the cinema.

One of the more frowned-upon trends was hire purchase. You could buy a refrigerator for half a crown (two shillings and sixpence) a week, a bedroom suite for one shilling a month; but a slightly feckless air hung about those who indulged in such extravagance.

The virtues of fresh air and exercise were extolled endlessly. Youth hostelling became very popular, and people went on hiking and biking holidays. Railway companies offered cheap fares and kitted out old carriages as camping coaches which were then parked in the country or by the sea. Visitors to holiday camps

increased and life generally began to be more fun for everybody. The prosperous joined in the fresh air fad; more and more people took up golf.

The women's League of Health and Beauty was formed and ladies wearing Greek tunics put on displays at fêtes and festivals. There was a great surge in the popularity of rugger, soccer and cricket.

It all helped to keep Britain healthy – which was just as well, as being ill was very expensive. A lot of self-prescribing went on – it was much cheaper to buy Fynnon Salts and Bile Beans than to get professional help.

If you went into a nursing home to have a baby it would cost you between £6 and £10; a pair of spectacles cost about six shillings and false teeth were a modest luxury. Children's illnesses often reached epidemic proportions and children were hospitalized for things like measles and whooping cough.

The Second World War did accomplish some good along with the evil – at least for the less well-off. Diet (despite food shortages) improved beyond all recognition; out of necessity food values were studied, the value of fresh vegetables was officially recognized, and people were issued with such life-improving goodies as extra vitamins and cod liver oil. As a result the nation was slimmer and fitter.

It had been well organized for the gathering storm. Thirty-eight million people had been issued with gas masks by the time war was declared (which proved mercifully unnecessary) and two million Anderson-type air raid shelters had been built (which proved very much the reverse). Armies of children were shipped off to the country to volunteer host families. Large country houses were commandeered for the war

The way to Britain's beauty

Penny-a-mile "Summer" Tickets by LMS

LONDON MIDLAND AND SCOTTISH RAILWAY

'Penny-a-Mile summer tickets' for holidaymakers were advertised by LMS, the London Midland and Scottish Railway.

Life-saving: instructions for using
a civilian gas mask, issued in
1940.

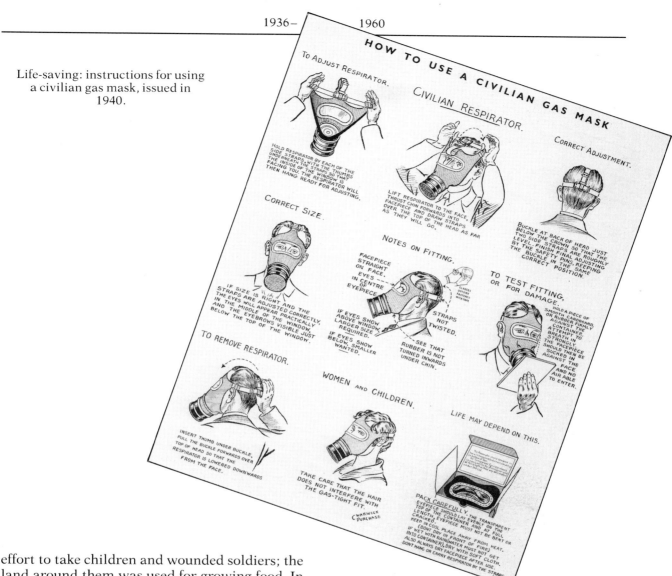

HOW TO USE A CIVILIAN GAS MASK

CIVILIAN RESPIRATOR.

To ADJUST RESPIRATOR.

HOLD RESPIRATOR BY EACH OF THE SIDE STRAPS WITH THE THUMBS UNDERNEATH THE STRAP SO THAT THE INSIDE OF THE WINDOW IS FACING YOU. THE RESPIRATOR WILL THEN HANG, READY FOR ADJUSTING.

LIFT RESPIRATOR TO THE FACE, THRUST CHIN FORWARDS INTO FACEPIECE AND DRAW STRAPS OVER THE TOP OF THE HEAD AS FAR AS THEY WILL GO.

CORRECT ADJUSTMENT.

BUCKLE AT BACK OF HEAD JUST BELOW THE CROWN SO THAT THE TWO SIDE STRAPS ARE ROUGHLY LEVEL. FINISH FINAL ADJUSTING BY THE SAFETY PINS, KEEPING THE BUCKLE IN THE SAME CORRECT POSITION

CORRECT SIZE.

IF SIZE IS RIGHT AND THE STRAPS ARE ADJUSTED CORRECTLY, THE EYES WILL APPEAR PRACTICALLY IN THE MIDDLE OF THE WINDOW, AND THE EYEBROWS VISIBLE JUST BELOW THE TOP OF THE WINDOW.

NOTES ON FITTING.

FACEPIECE STRAIGHT ON FACE. EYES IN CENTRE OF EYEPIECE

GLASSES (OUTSIDE) FASTEN WITH TAPE

IF EYES SHOW ABOVE WINDOW, LARGER SIZE REQUIRED. IF EYES SHOW BELOW, SMALLER WANTED.

STRAPS NOT TWISTED

SEE THAT RUBBER IS NOT TURNED INWARDS UNDER CHIN.

TO TEST FITTING, OR FOR DAMAGE.

HOLD A PIECE OF SMOOTH CARDBOARD, OR RUBBER FIRMLY AGAINST THE CONTAINER AND ATTEMPT TO BREATHE IN STRONGLY. THE FACEPIECE SHOULD THEN BE SUCKED IN AGAINST THE FACE AND NO AIR ABLE TO ENTER.

TO REMOVE RESPIRATOR.

INSERT THUMB UNDER BUCKLE, PULL THE BUCKLE FORWARDS OVER TOP OF HEAD SO THAT THE RESPIRATOR IS LOWERED DOWNWARDS FROM THE FACE.

WOMEN AND CHILDREN.

TAKE CARE THAT THE HAIR DOES NOT INTERFERE WITH THE GAS-TIGHT FIT.

LIFE MAY DEPEND ON THIS.

PACK CAREFULLY. THE TRANSPARENT EYEPIECE SHOULD LAY EVEN ON THE TOP OF THE CONTAINER AND AT FULL LENGTH. EYEPIECE MUST NOT BE BENT OR CRACKED. KEEP IN COOL PLACE AWAY FROM HEAT. (DONT DRY IN FRONT OF FIRE) IF WET WITH RAINWATER MUST NOT GET INTO CONTAINER, DRY WITH SOFT CLOTH. ALSO ALWAYS DRY FACEPIECE AFTER USE. DONT HANG OR CARRY RESPIRATOR BY THE STRAPS.

C WARWICK PURCHASE

effort to take children and wounded soldiers; the land around them was used for growing food. In the cities people Dug for Victory wherever a spade would go; Prince Albert found himself looking down from his memorial on to Kensington Gardens given over to allotments.

The streets of the cities were blacked out completely; brilliantly lit only by the bomb attacks. People who didn't have their own shelters, or who were out when the wailing sirens sounded, went literally underground and sheltered in the tube stations, emerging on the all-clear to find buildings shattered into rubble. Whole areas of London became unrecognizable, familiar landmarks completely wiped out.

Churchill became the embodiment of the British spirit of wartime resistance in his encouraging, cajoling and inspiring broadcasts.

Some of the most famous words of the twentieth century came over the wireless waves in his uplifting growl and the first patriotic memories of a whole generation were formed round the radio.

The Royal Family remained bravely at Buckingham Palace. After they had been bombed three times, Queen Elizabeth said she felt she could look the East End in the face. The big hotels were packed, 'like luxury liners', said *Vogue*, and in Grosvenor House a new deep-shelter restaurant was opened. Baths were offered to people instead of, or as well as, drinks.

Romance still flourished; war weddings were seen as a grab for happiness. Weekend-long honeymoons were either spent in borrowed country cottages or living dangerously in London which, in spite of everything, retained some kind of glamour. Church bells did not ring out for brides though, and there was a ban on rice-throwing.

There was one invasion of Britain during the war – of American GIs, dashing figures with pay many times that of the British soldiers. They stole British girls' hearts, and introduced gum, Coca Cola and jive to the nation. When the war was over about 80,000 GI Brides followed them back to America, anticipating a gilded future in a Hollywood-style home. The reality, however, was often more humble than what they left behind.

As the supply of even the most basic goods began to dwindle, people became more and more

TOP LEFT
A siren suit: utility clothing for women during the Second World War.

BOTTOM LEFT
The Royal Family bravely remained at Buckingham Palace throughout the war.

ingenious; you could hire hens by the week, join pig clubs and breed rabbits.

Utility clothing and furniture, with its unique trade mark, was the only kind on offer. Simple items like razor blades or toothbrushes became immensely desirable and the required daily reading of any housewife was her ration book. Budgeting food points became more difficult and crucial than juggling with money.

Towards the end of the war the spirits of the nation lifted for more than one reason; people looked forward to a new and better world. The Beveridge Report, upon which a new society was to be based with a new system of social security, sold 635,000 copies. The war had united everybody; it was felt that the old social barriers were down for good. Soldiers left the armed forces, exchanged their uniforms for demob suits and went confidently out to find a new world. It was a while coming to them. The country was very poor still and goods were in desperately short supply.

One of the more irritating sights which greeted people everywhere was the 'For Export Only' sign in shop windows. The villain of the hour was the spiv, in sharp suit, two-tone shoes and pencil-thin moustache, who could supply such exotica as nylons and bananas from the Black Market. The national occupation was queuing; you stood in line for everything.

Houses and ports had to be rebuilt; the desperate shortage of housing resulted in 'prefabs' – houses made section by section in factories and slotted together on site. They were not beautiful, but they were functional and warm. Forties architects planned high-rise flats; people went overboard for bungalows.

The basic petrol ration was abolished, but only essential motoring was allowed; Attlee, elected to power immediately after the war, saw economic recovery as his prime task.

People escaped, as always, via the radio and the cinema. Thirty-two million people went to the cinema every week; it was the age of the Ealing Comedy and the Great Romance (like *Brief Encounter*) with the occasional colour blockbuster like *Henry V*. On the radio worthy programmes like *The Brains Trust* joined the more cheery offerings like *ITMA* and *Take It From Here*.

The post-war elections were won on nationalization; it was all part of the much-heralded new social order. Electricity, gas, coal and the railways were all nationalized. In 1948, as part of the trend, the National Health Service was founded; medical care became a social right. As the economy recovered there was almost full employment, credit became more easily obtainable, and hire purchase was a simple fact of life.

'The modern miracle of television'

By 1950 there were 4.5 million cars in the country, and trailer caravans took to the roads. People moved around for pleasure in a way unimaginable to previous generations.

TV arrived. Critics claimed, with some justification, that it would ruin eyesight, interfere with homework and stop people talking to each other. It also, of course, broadened horizons, increased awareness and shrank the world.

A new breed was born in the 1950s. It was called The Teenager. It rocked, rolled, rebelled, and developed a sub-breed called the Teddy Boy.

Lady Docker drove around in her gold-plated, Zebra-upholstered Daimler and dazzled everybody. Liberace played the piano and out-dazzled even her, and towards the end of the Fifties the anti-hero was born, starring in kitchen sink drama. It was an interesting piece of social convolution – so many people had climbed socially so far into bland classlessness that there was a new status in the reality of genuine working-class origins. Actors (like Albert Finney and Marlon Brando) went about looking broody and sweaty instead of suave and smooth.

The big events of the early 1950s were the Coronation and the conquering of Everest, both fairy-tale triumphs gilding the decade with an almost tangible sense of victory, goodness and success, and a most marvellous antidote to the deprivation, misery and suffering of the war years. The Queen sat upon her throne and the Union Jack flew upon Everest and there was nothing which we patently could not do.

Two years earlier, the Festival of Britain had placed yet another jewel in the nation's crown; the Festival Hall and the Dome of Discovery drew millions of tourists to London. Designed to boost the country's morale, commemorate the Great Exhibition of 1851 and promote exports, it was a wild success on all counts.

Teenagers, 1950s style: a Teddy Boy in his velvet-collared Edwardian jacket dances with his girlfriend at a dance-hall.

WOMEN'S LOT

If the First World War had laid the foundations of female emancipation, the Second World War put up the walls and the Fifties saw the structure more or less complete.

The War equalized women socially perhaps even more than it did men. From 1940 onwards, single women and childless widows between 19 and 40 were liable for call-up. They could either join the services or work in factories. They were classed as 'mobile' and sent wherever they were needed, living in hostels. Much was asked of them, and they gave it, proving over and over again that they were as brave, competent and efficient as men.

Many women kept the family businesses going; others worked on the land or became mechanically adept. The WVS had nearly a million members, who ran canteens and rest centres, escorted evacuees and organized transport.

Working women had to do a set number of hours each week. They quite often made up the time doing two or three part-time jobs, running their families in odd moments in between.

Women's magazines like *Woman* and *Woman's Own* became extremely popular. Comparatively realistic in tone, they became the voice of the new woman, running articles on life in uniform alongside the recipes and child-care tips. All-women bands were popular, and played at first in uniform then later in glittering gowns under the inspired direction of Ivy Benson.

After the war harsh reality threatened women. Their menfolk returning from the Front took back the jobs they had left, and women were expected to return to hearth and home. Many women saw no reason to relinquish their freedom and their incomes.

Demands like equal pay for equal work were made and in the professions a long struggle began for economic equality. It wasn't until the late 1950s that teachers' salaries, for example, were properly adjusted.

And for the next generation, education and training for work outside the home was an automatic right. By the beginning of the 1960s, women were cabinet ministers, judges and doctors, and beginning to make themselves felt in industry. But it was progress bought at arguably high cost: some had relinquished security, respect and an absolutely clear position in society for stress, conflict and a high degree of self-doubt. Nevertheless, despite the problems, they liked life a great deal better that way.

DRESSED FOR IT

Fashion underwent a dramatic and bewildering series of changes during these twenty-five years. From the starting point of the mid-Thirties with their fluid feminine lines, clothes became functional and hard-edged during the war, extravagantly romantic immediately after it, and sharpened into the sleek stylish shape of the A-line and the shift dress as women advanced into the Sixties.

The war served one invaluable fashion purpose. As actress Judy Campbell pointed out, 'you could make lack of money look like lack of coupons'.

Fashion was getting ready for the war as the Thirties drew to a close. By 1938 skirts were shorter, headscarfs high fashion and the boiler suit an essential part of the wardrobe. By 1939, the sweater had become the basis for most looks for night and day, shirt dresses were being hailed for their undatable qualities and the uplift bra became one of life's necessities. For evening the

Forties jacket frocks: hair was worn in rolls, pleats and pincurls; make-up consisted of bright red lipstick.

shape was still long and clinging.

The silhouette of the war owed almost nothing to the influence of fashion and almost everything to the influence of uniform – short skirted, box pleated, square shouldered. Stockings became an unimaginable luxury, and such necessities as ankle socks and leg paint earned the 'fashion' label.

Purchase tax and lack of fabric forced economies on everybody – even *Vogue* gave advice on how to alter last year's look. The advice was scarcely necessary; changes were very slight. Make-up was hard, lips big and very red.

In 1940 silk stockings were actually banned, cosmetics virtually vanished, and women did their hair into rolls, pleats and pincurls. The flowing peekaboo 'Veronica Lake' hairstyle was banned in the factories for safety reasons, lest hair got caught in machinery.

The end of the war saw the freeing of Europe, the first jeans in *Vogue* (in 1946), and the New Look from Christian Dior (in 1947). Flowing skirts, flouncing petticoats, huge hats and high heels put women back into femininity. Women flirted with the New Look for a bit and then went into businesslike suits for their new businesslike lives in the Fifties.

Nylon made life easier, stockings sheerer and thick knits high fashion. Women wore their hair softly waved, their eyes heavily emphasized, and looked charmingly relaxed by day and immensely glamorous at night in wonderful off-the-shoulder crinoline dresses, as if to celebrate the heady, fairy-story mood of the Coronation era. In the late late Fifties, clothes became streamlined in shape and showed off the body in an immensely flattering way. The sack and the chemise dress made brief but bold headlines; the PVC raincoat was the new classic; shoes reached an all-time fantasy level in bead-encrusted satin, and hair was long and piled high.

Chanel relaunched navy blue and added pearls and camellias. St Laurent re-invented the leg; and a flurry of little girl-ish heroines (Hepburn, Bardot, Caron) heralded the youth revolution. Women looked wonderful; they were dressed for success.

ABOVE LEFT
Post-war evening wear: Hartnell's royal satin evening gown in kingfisher blue.

RIGHT
Fashion Fifties-style: by 1956 day clothes were charmingly relaxed.

ON THE HOME FRONT

Women's lives in the kitchen were also revolutionized during this quarter-century.

It wasn't until the mid-Thirties that real thought was given to the design of the kitchen. It was the poor relation of the house, often at the back or below ground level, with small windows and no view. This was a reflection of the low regard in which domestic servants were held – and if the household didn't run to servants, then any old place was still considered good enough for the lady of the house to labour away in. The main criterion was that it should be placed near the back door.

The cast iron stove dominated kitchens and cooking until well into the Thirties. It was still being installed in new houses after the war, although gas cooking was slowly becoming more acceptable. Electric stoves were long regarded with deep suspicion, largely because there was no visible source of heat. But by the mid-Thirties there was dial-control gas cooking, and a Baby Belling electric cooker could be bought for £4, or hired from the electricity company. These early cookers offered three heat settings – warm, medium and hot – and needed endless adjustment.

Cast-iron stoves dominated kitchens until well into the Thirties. But kitchens were soon revolutionized and by the Fifties gas and electric cookers and vacuum cleaners were common.

The refrigerator was still a rare commodity (only about 200,000 homes boasted one in 1939) and washing was done either by hand or in an electric wash boiler. Life was an endless round of daily shopping, weekly washing, ceaseless cooking and a great deal of washing up. But, after the war, women got a better deal in the kitchen as well as out in the world.

The sink unit and fitted kitchen first really saw the light of day in Fifties design. Planned to save labour rather than demand it, kitchens looked a bit like operating theatres, all glittering stainless steel, wipe-clean surfaces and easy-wash floors. The refrigerator at last became a standard fixture and the washing machine less of a luxury. Twin tubs came first (entailing a lot of very tedious transference from one tub to its twin) and then gradually, as the Fifties advanced, automatics began to take over. Dishwashers gained ground very slowly, partly through a predictable British puritanism, and partly for the more straightforward reason that some of the early models didn't wash the dishes very well.

The kitchen began to move from its exiled position at the back of the house. First the hatch, then the open plan 'kitchen-diner' and the decline of the dining room for family meals meant that the kitchen was moving to its true place at the heart of the house and of family life.

Detergents completely transformed washing and house cleaning, and cooking was becoming easier and easier. There were convenience foods (instant coffee, pie mixes) and frozen ones which could be stored in the fridge (and later the freezer, although it wasn't until the late Fifties that this wonder reached homes in Britain).

The pressure cooker also revolutionized cooking, particularly for women out at work all day. A stew could be ready in twenty minutes, potatoes in six. There was much less boiling of jam and preserving and pickling of fruit, and meal preparation had of necessity ceased to become a major chore.

It would all have seemed unimaginable to the housewife labouring over her range in 1910.

More storage space in less kitchen space: by the Fifties the refrigerator had become a standard fixture in kitchens at last.

THE BACKBONE OF BRITAIN

BY this time Oxo had become very much more than a food. It was part of the nation's gastronomic way of life alongside a nice cup of tea, and fish and chips. It was also hyper-famous; no name was more familiar, no brand better known than Oxo in its red and white packaging. It was an automatic part of every larder, additive to every recipe and addendum to every shopping list. It had passed into the language – it was not a type or brand of cooking aid or seasoning, but simply Oxo, an entity on its own.

There were major preoccupations in the country in the latter half of the Thirties; one was patriotism, the other sport. Oxo associated itself with both.

In 1935, for King George V's Jubilee, the Company's head office adorned itself (as befitted a Royal Warrant Holder) most elaborately, with the Oxo flag fluttering high above the building alongside the Union Jack and enough crowns, drapes, braid and bunting for the whole city of London.

The coronation of George VI in 1937 brought out a lot more; plus some charming souvenirs in the shape of red tin money boxes, price 6d. (for which you also got six cubes and a coronation leaflet). In coronation year, neatly managing to combine the two passions, Oxo published a 192-page *Games Guide to National Fitness*, both a reference book to world sporting records and a guide to the fundamentals of sport, with plenty of exhortation to the nation to get and stay fit. It was a great success.

The biggest loss to the Company for a long time came with the death of Lord Hawke in 1938. Lord Hawke was almost as integral a part of the Company as its packaging, particularly valued for his connections with the world of sport and healthy living. The visit to the Southwark factory of Sir William Arbuthnot Lane, Founder and President of the New Health Society, was one of the proudest moments of Hawke's career (made still prouder by Sir William's praise for the condition of the factory and the quality of its products).

Lord Hawke's company cricket team, and its annual match with the parent company Liebig's, was also very much part of the Oxo heritage. It was the chairman of Liebig's, K.M. Carlisle, who took Lord Hawke's place and saw the Company safely and productively through the Second World War.

Flying the flag: Oxo's head offices in the City of London adorned in celebration of King George V's Jubilee in 1935.

Each 6ᵈ Tin Contains 6 OXO Cubes and Coronation Leaflet

Coronation souvenirs.

ABOVE
Red tin money-boxes.

RIGHT
A paper Oxo crown.

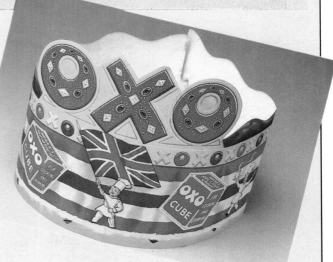

THE FLAVOUR OF LIFE

Many people were still poor in the Thirties – very poor. Oxo did its bit to help them. A lot of bleak unsatisfying diets were made a bit warmer, more comforting and more flavoursome by the addition of the cube here and there. A sad little story appeared in the *Northamptonshire Evening Telegraph*, telling of a 'pitiful widower of 85' making ends meet somehow on ten shillings a week. Along with one piece of meat for the week and half a pint of milk, he listed one penny square of Oxo 'to be eked out for three nights for supper'. That such an economy was even possible is at once shocking and astounding.

On a slightly more indulgent level, it was recorded in the *United Service Review* that for crews of aircraft engaged on flights of four or more hours' duration, there was a meal allowance of threepence a head for Oxo 'or equivalent beverage'. But who would want such a thing? In such small but crucial ways was the patriotic image of Oxo formed and reformed, and its nourishing qualities come to be taken totally for granted.

Thirties and Forties Oxo advertising concentrated on the Cube's goodness and value for money.

FIGHTING FIT

And then the war came. It was clear that no London factory was going to survive for very long and the Oxo company (along with many others) removed its factories from the capital and out to Wiltshire and a disused cotton mill in Lancashire.

The women workers there, trained for generations to work on looms, switched their skills to cube manufacture and packaging. They adapted far more easily than the premises, which had been constructed to maintain the very humid conditions suited to cotton production. Air conditioning had to be installed and a much higher standard of hygiene maintained. The Company, being what it was, managed both, and production soared.

It needed to. During the war Oxo was one of the very few flavoursome things around. Recipe after recipe for such ingenious-sounding dishes as Allotment Pie and Potage Villageois included Oxo among their ingredients. Cooks' ingenuity was challenged by dishes such as these featured in *The Sketch*: Sardines au Riz and Cataif aux Pommes. Their ingredients were few and sparse, and consisted of a great deal of water and very small portions of the other things. Potage Villageois must have owed almost all its flavour to the three Oxo cubes it recommends: otherwise consisting as it did of 4 slices of bacon, 2 pints of water and a pound of Jerusalem artichokes. Nevertheless, the nation survived to tell the tale.

Oxo was also constantly recommended as an additive to such wartime indelicacies as dried eggs, dripping and boiling bones. The cook was assured that the flavour 'will be very much improved'. It needed to be.

Oxo was a vital food for the troops in the war, an essential part of their diet, but it was perhaps more on the home than on the battle front that

Oxo helped in its small way to win the war. Hundreds of thousands of cups and flasks of its tasty comforting warmth accompanied people into their shelters, on Home Guard Duty and in community centres and emergency establishments – bringing a touch of normality, home and comfort to the bleak miseries of a besieged nation.

One of the more historic and intriguing uses to which the Oxo tins were put during the war was in the Channel Islands. The Nazis had con-

Digging for victory: a Second World War advertisement.

fiscated all wireless sets (lest the inspirational tones of Winston Churchill or cheering news from the BBC might boost islanders' morale), but an ingenious pair of mechanics called Harold Rive and Louis Roche manufactured over 2,000 miniature crystal sets, so small that Oxo tins could and did house them, safely concealed from the enemy's eyes.

HEADLINE HITTING

After the war, when food was still both extremely scarce and extremely dull, housewives turned to Oxo not just to add flavour but to provide it. When a Mrs Mellor of Manchester caused a national furore by claiming in the *Daily Despatch* that she managed to give her husband and two children four good meals a day and make a joint last four meals, scores of disbelieving housewives demanded to know how she did it and wondered if perhaps 'four Oxo cubes equalled four square meals'? As an advertising slogan it would have worked well.

The boat race crews in 1948, described by their coaches as 'nothing like so well nourished' as in pre-war days, were looking for methods of supplementing the normal food ration. Oxford were importing whale-meat steaks; Cambridge settled for a 'hot cup of meat extract immediately after rowing'. Oxo was back in the sports business with a vengeance.

Oxo also hit the headlines with a report of young mothers and old people virtually on starvation rations, supper consisting simply of 'one Oxo cube'. And this was not during the war years, but in 1948. What they would all have done if there had been no Oxo is depressing to contemplate.

Oxo's claim to the title of the Penny Cube was finally lost in 1952. Until then it appeared constantly in family budgets and nostalgic articles about What You Can Still Buy For A Penny. In 1951 that consisted of a small packet of chewing gum, a small toffee and the Cube; in 1952 not even that. Oxo was sevenpence halfpenny for six and history had been made – or at least rewritten.

A bizarre little matter got Oxo into the House of Commons in Coronation year. During a heated exchange over food bonuses for the Coronation Mrs Jean Mann (Labour, Coatbridge and Airdrie)

Do mothers starve to feed their children?

RATION TEST IN VILLAGE

MOTHERS with growing families are next on the list for a Ministry of Food rations inquiry by practical tests, to be conducted in the village of Drinkstone, Suffolk (pop. 377).

The Ministry has ordered its dieticians to investigate reports that the health of young mothers is suffering because, unable to make the rations go far enough, they are starving themselves to feed their children.

The "old folks rations quiz" at Felsham, in the same district, closed yesterday and the investigators despatched reports to the Ministry.

They give particulars of every item of food eaten by 20 old folk during the past week. At the Ministry each food list will be translated into calories and compared with the minimum calory figure upon which the Ministry bases the whole ration system.

Her three meals

Typical of the entries is that of Mrs. Ellen Homex, whose report for one day was : Breakfast, 1 slice of bread, butter, 2 cups of tea, milk, 1 teaspoon sugar. Dinner : Chop, greens, and potatoes, 1 slice of bread. Tea : 2 slices of bread and margarine, jam, 2 cups of tea. Supper : 1 Oxo cube.

The Ministry has not finished yet with the old folk of Felsham. A Whitehall doctor is now to be sent to examine them "from the clinical standpoint."

Each Drinkstone mother of children over five years old will be issued with forms and a pair of scales and will note down the weight and kind of food she eats at every meal.

TOP
It's Oxo: 1948 Easter Monday van parade in London's Regent's Park.

ABOVE
Post-war rations: supper for some people in 1948 consisted solely of one Oxo cube.

asked where an ox could be obtained for roasting traditional style, in the street on the great day. 'Roast Oxo Cubes,' cried Members loyally and wittily. (It is not recorded whether oxen were ever found.)

Rising prices: the Penny Cube finally became extinct in 1952.

TOP OF THE WORLD

1953 saw Oxo literally on top of the world, as John Hunt and his team took the Cube up Everest with them. It is extraordinarily pleasing to picture the Cube up there on the summit, its staunch red and white alongside the red, white and blue.

On the day the news of Everest's conquest reached London, Queen Elizabeth II was crowned. It was the wettest June day for years and cold with it, but still people slept on the pavements to be sure of a good view. Oxo was out there patriotically with them, in Thermos flasks by the thousands. I can personally vouch for at least one Thermos full of the stuff going off to the Mall with my cousins.

GIVING IT AWAY

Among the famous gifts from Oxo during this period was a series of painting books for children. A strong moral tone was conveyed throughout: one was entitled *Good Manners*, showing (on the cover) two evidently exquisitely-behaved children gazing up with respectful adoration at their father. *Paint the ABC of Health and Fitness* was another, showing a mass of healthy sportspeople; and *Mother Earth, She Feeds and Clothes Us* was yet another stirring title, with a smiling earth carrying a cornucopia of fruit and vegetables in her arms, while beside her stood a herd of patient cattle with their inevitable connotations of Oxo. The Oxo child was being well instructed.

For the grown-ups there were kitchen utensils, and, as the craze for photography spread, and the Box Brownie made its debut, 'a free enlargement of your favourite snapshot'.

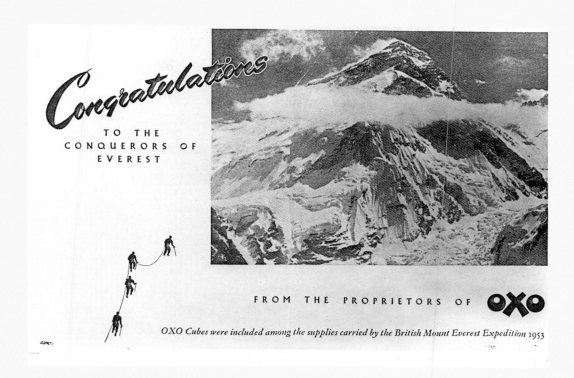

ABOVE
Conquering Everest: the 1953
British Mount Everest Expedition
took the Cube with them.

RIGHT
Edmund Hillary (left), Sherpa
Tensing (right) and Colonel Hunt
(centre) take a last look at the
mountain they have just
conquered.

It is immensely intriguing to look back to these early 'offers', and note that they have only changed in form. The wonders of the computer have made their administration easier; but although the faces in the painting books may have a futuristic look about them these days and the kitchen utensils may have become slightly more sophisticated, the basic marketing ideas are exactly the same.

Good manners: one of a series of painting books for children given away during this period.

TELLING AND SELLING

Oxo's advertising entered a major new era during this quarter-century – the television commercial. Television had taken over the country's mass culture, and now it took over its advertising. Every product had to learn to adapt to, and indeed exploit, the new medium. Oxo had never been slow to learn. Its advertising had always been ahead of its time, and it took to the small screen with immense flair and skill.

Meanwhile, back in the mid-Thirties, it was at a slightly less sophisticated stage.

Between the wars there was a craze for plays on words. Oxo's loyal public were invited to send in slogans, the best of which appeared on the hoardings and in the press. Such literary gems as 'Greta colday with a cup of hot oxo', and 'Willie B Hardy? Yes – if he takes Oxo', attained immortality. This was followed by a slightly more intellectual theme as in 'William the Conqueror 1066 AD; Oxo 11.15am.'

The whole campaign served two purposes admirably: it hammered the Oxo brand name firmly home, and it kept people thinking about it,

LEFT
Paint the ABC of Health and Fitness: inspiring children to lead healthy lives with the help of Oxo.

BELOW
Playing on words: in the Thirties the public were invited to send Oxo their slogans, the best of which were used in advertising.

as they tried to invent new slogans of their own.

Limericks were another craze: you could win £1,000 for a really good one. A sexist tone is to be found in one of the winners:

If hubby is heard to ask 'Why
Is this meat so infernally dry?'
Get some Oxo and look
In your cookery book
And incipient squalls will all fly.

The message was clear (and was put into several more campaigns later on): if you want to keep your man happy, give him Oxo.

During the war the advertising became simple, stark and hugely effective. 'On a plane by itself', read one, showing the Cube sitting boldly on the wing of a plane escorted by Hurricanes in full battle flight. 'Sow. . . Grow. . . then *ADD* Oxo', said another, showing a pile of vegetables and a diligent allotmenteer. 'Just time for an Oxo', says a serviceman breezily to a service lady outside a refreshments area in a crowded station.

The benefit to children continued to be a very strong theme: 'Oxo for the children's welfare', 'Oxo keeps him fit', and 'Good night children

Wartime advertising became simple, stark and very effective.

everywhere' (with a picture of two angelic children clutching their bedtime drinks).

Later the slogans became slightly more sophisticated: 'The essential ingredient', 'Oxo works wonders' and 'Oxo keeps you glowing'. Some curiosities found their way into the campaigns: 'It's an odd house where there's no Oxo' declared one ad., the copy set around a crooked house. Odder still was a small Scottish boy in outgrown kilt and sporran, weeping. 'Puir wee laddie. Ma mither winna gie me ony mair

Oxo. It mak's me grow oot o' my claes,' he tells his understandably puzzled Scottie dog.

By the mid-Fifties the television commercial had arrived. Oxo's first was an earnest effort, showing an endless army of cubes marching behind the Oxo banner. 'Millions of Cubes' was the rather uninspired message. A couple of years later creativity had soared and Oxo was being sold by Sooty, the most popular glove puppet of the time. During one of the early years of commercial television 52 Sooty commercials were

produced so a different one could be shown every week.

Meanwhile in the press, sexism was alive and doing well. 'Oxo gives a meal man-appeal', cried the now-famous headline over a picture of a girl merrily nearly dropping a casserole dish, while behind her a manly chap appeared to be about to grab her. It was brilliant stuff, totally in tune with the times; the girl might have been trying to please her man, but she was also clearly glamorous, intelligent and fun.

And so, very much in that same mould, as the Fifties drew to a close, one of the most famous characters ever to emerge out of advertising was born – Katie. Katie and Oxo were to become synonymous over the next two decades. But even by the early dawn of 1960, she was established as believable, attractive and interesting – and the housewives of Britain took her to their hearts.

During this period advertising was transformed and as usual Oxo was leading the way – whether with effective wartime posters, Sooty in the early years of commercial television or Katie in the late Fifties.

RECIPES

LIFE was interrupted once again during this period by the outbreak of the Second World War. People's ingenuity was sorely tested, due to the general shortages caused by severe rationing, and it was amazing what could be done with the meagre allowance of meat. The food was far from memorable, but successfully fed a hungry population. Whale meat, spam and dried egg powder were introduced into the national diet and vegetables were home-grown.

CHESTNUT STEW
(issued in 1939)

The chestnuts can be gathered from your local wood, making this a very economical dish.

SERVES 4

1lb (450g) fresh or dried sweet chestnuts
2 onions
4 mushrooms
1 carrot
1 leek
2 tbs butter or margarine
parsley, thyme and bay leaf
1 red Oxo cube dissolved in ½pt (300ml) hot water

If dried chestnuts are used, soak overnight and drain. Slice the vegetables and fry them gently in the butter or margarine until brown. Put in a stew pan with the chestnuts, herbs, seasoning and Oxo stock. Simmer gently over a low heat for 2 hours.

POTAGE VILLAGEOIS
(issued in 1942)

SERVES 4

4 slices of bacon
½lb (225g) Jerusalem artichokes
2 red Oxo cubes dissolved in 2 pts (1 litre) boiling water

Cut the bacon into small squares. Fry them lightly in their own fat. Peel and wash artichokes, cut them in half and put them, with the bacon, into boiling Oxo stock. Leave for twenty minutes, off the heat. Reheat before serving.

COLLOPS OF TINNED MEAT
(issued in 1943)

Croutons, made of toast or fried bread, make a tasty accompaniment to this dish.

SERVES 4

1 12oz (350g) tin of meat (any kind)
1 onion
1 tbs cooking fat
1 tbs flour
1 red Oxo cube dissolved in 1 pt (600ml) hot water
2 tbs of mushroom ketchup or Yorkshire relish
salt and pepper

Cut the meat into dice or neat slices. Peel and slice the onion. Melt the fat in a pan, put in the onion and flour and fry until brown. Add the Oxo stock, ketchup or relish and the seasoning and stir till the mixture boils. Add the meat and let it simmer in the gravy over a low heat for about half an hour.

ALLOTMENT PIE
(issued in 1945)

SERVES 4–6

2 cupfuls cooked potatoes
2 cupfuls cooked vegetables, e.g. beans, peas, carrots, cabbage
2oz (50g) cooking fat
1 red Oxo cube dissolved in ¼pt (150ml) hot water
1 cooked onion
salt and pepper
½lb (225g) pastry

Cut the cooked potatoes into small cubes and chop the rest of the vegetables, except the peas, coarsely. Heat the fat in a pan, put in the vegetables and stir for a few minutes, taking care that they do not brown. Add Oxo stock to the vegetables and season to taste. Put all into a pie-dish. Roll out the pastry, and lay a narrow strip round the top of the dish, having first brushed the edge with a little water. Put on a lid made of the pastry, pressing the edges well together. Decorate the edges with a fork, and the top with leaves of pastry. Bake in a moderate oven (375°F, 190°C, gas mark 5) until the pastry has risen. Brush the top with a little beaten egg before it is baked for a more attractive effect.

BRISKET AND LEEK POT ROAST

This traditional combination should be cooked until it is tender.

SERVES 6

2lb (900g) brisket
1 tbs flour
1oz (25g) cooking fat
4oz (100g) onion, chopped
4oz (100g) turnip, peeled and chopped
1 red Oxo cube dissolved in ¼pt (150ml) hot water
1½lb (675g) leeks, washed and diced

Dust the meat with flour. Heat the fat in a large flameproof casserole and quickly fry the meat on both sides. Remove it from casserole. Add the onion and turnip to the fat. Cover with the lid; cook over a low heat for 10 minutes, stirring occasionally. Drain off the fat and return the meat to the pan. Pour the Oxo stock over the meat, cover and cook at 325°F, 160°C, gas mark 3 for about 1½ hours. Add the leeks to the casserole and cook for further half-hour. Skim off the excess fat from juices before serving.

TRADITIONAL STEAK AND KIDNEY PUDDING

If this is made in a pressure cooker then Oxo has a double use – it not only makes good gravy with the meat, but also provides the added flavour which is needed with quick cooking.

SERVES 4–6

1lb (450g) steak, cut into 1-inch (3-cm) cubes
3 tbs flour
1 tsp salt
¼ tsp pepper
½lb (225g) kidney, skinned and cored
¾lb (375g) suet pastry (8oz/225g flour, 3oz/75g suet)
2 onions, peeled and sliced
1 red Oxo cube dissolved in ¼pt (150ml) water

Toss the steak in the flour, seasoned with the salt and pepper. Cut the kidney into small pieces. Make the pastry. Use a 1½pt to 2pt (900 to 1200ml) size basin. Roll the pastry to line it, keeping enough for the lid. Put in the meat and onions in layers, add the Oxo stock to come half-way up the meat, cover with the pastry lid and press the edges together. Cover with a cloth or aluminium foil and secure with string. Steam for 3 to 4 hours (longer cooking improves the pudding). Serve in the basin.

AMERICAN MINCEMEAT LOAF

Serve this loaf sliced with hot Oxo gravy.

SERVES 4–6

1 tbs cooking fat
1 small onion, chopped
1lb (450g) lean stewing or braising meat, minced (not leg or shin)
1½oz (40g) fresh breadcrumbs or rolled oats
garlic clove, chopped (optional)
1 tsp salt
¼ tsp pepper
¼ tsp ground mace or nutmeg
chopped fresh or dried herbs to taste
1 red Oxo cube dissolved in ¼pt (100ml) hot water
flour for dusting

Heat the fat and gently fry the onion until it is light brown and soft (about 10 minutes). Place in a mixing bowl with the rest of the ingredients (except the stock and flour) and mix well. Add sufficient Oxo stock to bind the mixture. Turn the meat mixture on to a floured board and shape it into a loaf about 2in (5cm) deep. Place this in a greased roasting tin, cover with parchment paper and bake at 375°F, 190°C, gas mark 5 for ¾ to 1 hour. Remove the paper for the last 10 minutes to brown the loaf.

BACON HOT POT

The mustard and treacle give this traditional favourite a barbeque flavour.

SERVES 4

1½lb (675g) piece of bacon, soaked
1 large onion, peeled and sliced
2 stalks celery, chopped
½ tsp mustard
¼ tsp pepper
2 tbs black treacle
2 red Oxo cubes dissolved in ¾pt (450ml) hot water
½lb (225g) soaked butter beans or 1 small can butter beans

Cut the bacon into four pieces, put them into a casserole and add the onion and celery. Mix the mustard, pepper and treacle with the Oxo stock and pour this over the meat and vegetables. Cook covered at 300°F, 150°C, gas mark 2 for 2 hours. Add the drained butter beans and cook for a further hour.

KIDNEYS SAUTÉ

This original kidney dish is light enough as a starter if served in small helpings.

SERVES 2

4 lamb's kidneys, halved, skinned and cored
1 tbs flour, seasoned
1 tbs cooking fat
½oz (12g) butter or margarine
1 red Oxo cube dissolved in ¼pt (150ml) hot water
1 tbs white wine vinegar
¼ tsp ground ginger
1 tsp brown sugar
2oz (50g) stoned raisins
freshly boiled long grain rice
chopped parsley for garnish

Cut each half kidney into two and toss in the seasoned flour. Heat the fat and add the butter or margarine and kidneys and sauté gently for 3 minutes. Add the Oxo stock to the kidneys with the vinegar, ginger, sugar and raisins. Bring to the boil; simmer for 10 minutes. Serve on a bed of rice; sprinkle the dish generously with chopped parsley.

LIVER RISOTTO

This delicious risotto can be used as a stuffing in baked tomatoes or in an omelette.

SERVES 2–3

2oz (50g) cooking fat
3oz (75g) onion, chopped
6oz (175g) patna rice or long grain rice
2 red Oxo cubes dissolved in 1pt (600ml) hot water
1oz (25g) bacon, derinded and chopped
½oz (12g) butter or margarine
4oz (100g) lamb's liver, washed and diced small
2oz (50g) canned or cooked sweet red pepper, sliced
salt and pepper
2oz (50g) Cheddar cheese, grated

Heat the fat in a heavy pan and fry the onion until it begins to brown. Add the rice and cook for a further 3 minutes. Remove from the heat and add the hot Oxo stock. Stir well and bring to boil. Cover and simmer gently for 15 to 20 minutes until all the stock is absorbed. Meanwhile fry the bacon in the butter or margarine then lightly fry the liver. Add this to the cooked rice together with the red pepper, and heat well, seasoning to taste. Serve the cheese separately.

1961~1985

TO THE PRESENT DAY

BRINGING history to the present day is always an astonishing process; so much seems to happen with bewildering speed, and very recently, too. Events which took place over twenty years ago seem like yesterday's headlines; and yet comparing the news now with that of 75 years ago, there is surprisingly (and soberingly) little change. People's spirit of adventure, courage and creativity continues as we look forward into the 21st century.

1961

John Fitzgerald Kennedy was inaugurated as the 35th President of the United States; Yuri Gagarin became the first person to orbit the earth; and a dividing wall was built to curb the flow of refugees from East to West Berlin. *Breakfast at Tiffany's* and *Jules et Jim* were the films not to be missed.

1962

Glenn and Scott went into orbit in a US rocket; US Telstar 1, the first active communications satellite, was launched; the US blockaded Cuba over Russian missile sites; and Marilyn Monroe died. The first report on smoking and health was published; centigrade was first used for weather forecasts; and *Private Eye* and *That Was The Week That Was* brought satire to Britain.

1963

Hugh Gaitskell died; Harold Wilson became leader of the Labour Party; De Gaulle refused Britain entry into the Common Market; and the Great Train Robbery of £2.5 million thrilled and shocked at the same time. Sir Alec Douglas-Home became Conservative Prime Minister succeeding Macmillan; and the Profumo scandal rocked the country. In November, Kennedy was assassinated in Dallas.

1964

BBC2 first opened; licences were granted to drill for oil in the North Sea; Labour won the General Election and Harold Wilson became Prime Minister. Martin Luther King won the Nobel Peace Prize; Lyndon Johnson won the US presidential election. C.P. Snow's *The Corridors of Power* was published; and the *Sun* replaced the *Daily Herald*.

1965

Sir Winston Churchill died; Edward Heath became Leader of the Conservative Party; Elizabeth Lane was appointed the first woman High Court judge; and Radio Caroline and other private radio stations hit the high seas. 3,500 US marines landed in Vietnam; the first oil strike was made in the North Sea; and the death penalty was abolished for murder.

1966

England won the World Cup; a six-month freeze on wages, salaries and prices was announced; Francis Chichester set sail round the world; and pandas Chi-Chi and An-An met in Moscow. Britain's first Polaris submarine was launched; and the Aberfan disaster shocked the world.

1967

Francis Chichester arrived in Plymouth; Jeremy Thorpe was elected Leader of the Liberal Party; Moshe Dayan was appointed Israel's Defence Minister and the Six-Day War broke out in the Middle East. The pound was devalued; and colour television first came to our screens, on BBC2. The first human heart transplant operation was carried out at Cape Town in South Africa.

1968

Martin Luther King and Senator Robert Kennedy were both assassinated; and Richard Nixon won the US presidential election. Censorship in the theatre was abolished in the Theatres Act, and *Hair* arrived on the London stage. The two-tier postal system began in Britain; and *M*A*S*H* was the definitive film.

1969

Golda Meir became Prime Minister of Israel; General de Gaulle resigned; and Prince Charles's Investiture as Prince of Wales at Caernarvon Castle took place. Neil Armstrong was the first man to land on the moon; the army took over policing and security in Northern Ireland; British-built Concorde had her maiden flight; and the voting age became 18.

1970

The Tories came back into power; de Gaulle died; and the *New English Bible* and *The Female Eunuch* by Germaine Greer were published. *The Rocky Horror Show* and Peter Brook's *A Midsummer Night's Dream* made theatrical history in their different ways.

1971

The Open University first went on the air, Rolls Royce Ltd collapsed and decimal currency was introduced to Britain. Indira Gandhi had a landslide victory in the Indian general election, and a direct telephone link between Britain and China was opened after 22 years.

1972

The miners went on strike, resulting in large-scale powercuts, and a state of emergency was declared. Five burglars were caught in the Watergate Building in Washington D.C., USA, the Democratic Party's campaign headquarters. Ken Russell made Twiggy a star in *The Boy Friend* and, in total contrast, directed The Who's rock opera, *Tommy*.

1973

A cease-fire agreement was signed and the last American soldier left Vietnam. Dr Henry Kissinger became US Secretary of State and President Nixon denied all knowledge of the Watergate burglary. Princess Anne married Mark Phillips, and Britain (with Ireland and Denmark) became a member of the EEC.

1974

Direct rule by the British government in Northern Ireland ended for five months; the three-day week and the miners' strike resulted in the collapse of the Tory government and Heath's resignation, and a minority Labour government took office. The IRA bombed the Tower of London and two Birmingham bars. Giscard d'Estaing became President of France; and President Nixon resigned, Gerald Ford taking over in his place.

1975

The Vietnam War ended; Margaret Thatcher was elected Leader of the Conservative Party; the Education Bill was published making comprehensive school education compulsory; and the Sex Discrimination and Equal Pay Acts came into force. *The Towering Inferno* was one of the first disaster movies to appear.

1976

Harold Wilson resigned and Jim Callaghan became Prime Minister. Princess Margaret and Lord Snowdon announced their separation, and Jeremy Thorpe resigned from the Liberal Party, David Steel taking his place. The Israeli raid on Entebbe airport took place; the first oil from the Brent North Sea oilfield was refined; the National Theatre opened; and Concorde started passenger service. Jimmy Carter was elected US President.

1977

The Lib-Lab pact was made; and the firemen went on strike. In South Africa there was a crackdown on anti-apartheid groups; and President Sadat of Egypt made his historic address to the Israeli Knesset in Jerusalem. Britain and the Commonwealth celebrated the Queen's Silver Jubilee.

1978

In Britain inflation was down to single figures; the first May Day holiday was celebrated; and the world's first test-tube baby, Louise Brown, was born in Oldham, Lancashire. Soviet dissidents Ginsberg and Shcharansky were sentenced to long-term imprisonment in Russia; 346 Vietnamese boat people arrived in Britain; and the world's birthrate dropped to the lowest level in recorded history.

1979

The Shah left Iran and Ayatollah Khomeini, the Muslim leader, returned from exile, an Islamic Republic being declared in April. Margaret Thatcher won the general election and became Britain's first woman Prime Minister; and Earl Mountbatten was murdered. Mother Theresa won the Nobel Peace Prize; and the first heart transplant operation in Britain was carried out at Papworth Hospital near Cambridge.

1980

Rhodesia became the independent nation of Zimbabwe; Ronald Reagan won the US presidential election; and John Lennon was shot dead in New York. Michael Foot became the new leader of the Labour Party; the Mini Metro was launched; Sebastian Coe and Steve Ovett continually broke running records; and the Queen Mother celebrated her 80th birthday.

1981

Prince Charles and Lady Diana Spencer announced their engagement and were married on 29 July. Blanks were fired at the Queen during the Trooping of the Colour; the Yorkshire Ripper was convicted; and the first London Marathon was run. The US Space Shuttle Columbia was launched; Solidarity held their first national congress in Gdansk, Poland; Francois Mitterand won the French presidential election; and Greece joined the EEC. The launch of the SDP was announced, and the Liberal-SDP alliance was formed.

1982

The Falkland Islands War was fought between Britain and Argentina; Prince William of Wales was born; the Tudor warship Mary Rose was raised from beneath the sea; Channel 4 TV opened; and unemployment reached three million people while annual inflation was at its lowest level for ten years. The Commonwealth Games opened in Brisbane, Australia.

1983

The US Pioneer 10 spacecraft became the first man-made object to travel beyond the solar system; Lech Walesa won the Nobel Peace Prize; and there was a massive bomb explosion outside Harrods in London. Breakfast TV began in Britain; the £1 coin was introduced; David Owen became the leader of the SDP and Neil Kinnock the leader of the Labour Party while the Conservatives were re-elected in the general election. Lady Donaldson became the first woman Lord Mayor of London; and the British-made film *Gandhi* won eight Oscars.

1984

The first free flight in space took place from the Space Shuttle Challenger; Prince Harry of Wales was born; and Mrs Gandhi was killed, her son Rajiv becoming the new Prime Minister of India. Jayne Torvill and Christopher Dean won the ice dancing gold medal at the winter Olympics; WPC Yvonne Fletcher was shot dead outside the Libyan Embassy in London; and the miners' strike against pit closures began.

1985

The miners' strike ended after a year of great bitterness; the pound sunk to a record low against the US dollar; Ethiopia suffered acute famine; and the Allies celebrated the fortieth anniversary of VE Day. *Amadeus*, *A Passage to India* and *The Killing Fields* scooped up most of the Oscars between them; and the Oxo cube celebrated its 75th Diamond Jubilee!

THE COMPUTER AGE

BETWEEN 1961 and 1985, the whole pace of life changed; the world seemed to spin faster on its axis. Oil suddenly became a subject of overwhelming importance, and terms like the 'New Technology' and 'silicon chip'

We can work it out: the Beatles during rehearsals for the Royal Variety Command Performance in 1963.

passed into everyone's vocabulary, changed the present, and transformed the future.

Human beings, who only fifty years earlier had been perfecting the motor car, landed on the moon; and the only thing that rose faster than inter-planetary rockets were prices. It was the quarter-century that invented inflation, swinging London, mini skirts and the Beatles, flower power, property booms and overnight fortunes. You could hardly catch on to one aspect of the new world before everything changed again. Holidays abroad, two-car families and credit-style living became totally commonplace; and yet poverty and rising unemployment still lurked perpetually beneath the surface.

The Sixties in particular were a very difficult time of adjustment for anybody who had been an adult during the war. It was the age of youth. Experience and wisdom were no longer considered as important as vitality, lateral thinking and creativity. In fashion, music and popular philosophy, young people were wildly successful, making fortunes overnight, collecting the adulation of millions, and courted by their elders and betters in search of the New Wisdom in the media. The power of the popular hero or heroine was breathtaking; a word from A Beatle or Ms Quant was considered of interest to half the nation.

It was also the age of the sexual revolution. The Pill had completely changed the attitude of young people, young women in particular, to sex. With the fear of pregnancy gone, many of the old moral attitudes faded. Homosexuality was legalized, there was nude bathing and the divorce rate soared.

The early part of the decade was breathtakingly prosperous. There was virtually full employment and making a fortune was, if not easy, very possible indeed – given a good idea, the

Mary Quant, one of the starry names of the Swinging Sixties.

willingness to work hard and the ability to present yourself.

That was crucial. This was the media age – now with us forever – when to be able to talk well, to create an image, put yourself across was suddenly as important as what you had to say and what you were saying it about. Every area of human life – literally – was to be seen on the screen. Mostly the small one, but activities that were considered truly unsuitable for the living room could be shown, with an X certificate, on the large one.

The starry names of the Sixties would have filled a firmament: The Beatles, the Rolling Stones, Mary Quant, Vidal Sassoon. What was interesting was that the idols were all – or to a large extent – English. The world flocked to London to learn to live the modern way.

Satire was a reflection of the irreverence of the age; television programmes like *That Was the Week That Was*, revues like *Beyond the Fringe* and magazines like *Private Eye* relentlessly mocked leaders.

But towards the end of the decade the sky darkened. There was a staggering increase in world commodity prices. The cost of petrol went up five-fold, and took everything with it. Redundancies and cutbacks became as common as prosperity had been before. So did inflation. Prices went up and up. As a result strikes for higher pay, even by the dedicated professions – nurses and firemen – occurred frequently. By 1975, the value of money was roughly a fifth of what it had been thirty years before. Measures like wage freezes, credit squeezes, prices and income boards and reductions in state expenditure were introduced to try to cope with the spiralling inflation.

The price of houses went into orbit. Fortunes in property were made rapidly. The darker side was a lack of accommodation for people unable to buy their own homes. A few were driven on to the street by 'Rachmanism' – a peculiarly nasty form of harrassment by landlords, named after Peter Rachman who perfected a method of terrorizing tenants out of their homes, and gave landlords as a whole an unfair and appalling name.

Advances in technology were almost unbelievable. The silicon chip changed the face and function of science. The most complex computer was reduced to the size of a typewriter, and could help build cars, type letters, diagnose simple diseases and instruct pupils. A computer could store shelfloads of information on one floppy disk, and a calculator could do hours' work in minutes. None of which helped unemployment – which is still a problem many of us face today. Nuclear power, albeit a solution to the world's energy crisis, was considered by

Minis were socially desirable as well as practical and economical.

MINIS. You just can't feel that way about any other car –when everything else goes wrong your Mini will still love you. Austin-Morris MINIS from £573 (inc. tax). AUSTIN MORRIS

some to be a threat as well as a blessing. Solar, wind and sea power were all hopefully investigated as alternatives. The fear of nuclear war hung over humanity.

Concern for the environment grew, alongside the developments that would wreck it. Environmental groups sprung up, conducting campaigns to protect the countryside, the water, the air. People became interested in the effect of food additives and chemical fertilizers on their diet; health food shops appeared in the high streets. One of the best things about the Seventies and Eighties was that people became a little less bothered about themselves in particular, and a little more concerned about mankind in general.

The fuel crisis changed the motor industry. Small economic cars were not only practical, they were also socially desirable. All the manufacturers were competing in a race for more mpg rather than for more mph. The humble bicycle got a new lease of life, being not only cheaper and more ecologically sound than a car, but also healthier and more in keeping with the nation's new obsession with the pursuit of fitness. Jogging, yoga and aerobics had by the Eighties become part of national life.

The advances in medicine were extraordinary. Diseases like pneumonia, TB, typhoid and diphtheria, which had been mass killers, were brought under control by modern drugs, though cancer continues to stalk the earth and AIDS is a new terror.

Television became more and more of an influence; it decimated cinema audiences, dominated conversation, changed thinking and became a common topic of talk. It also changed the nature of newspapers which, deprived of their function to be first with the news, became much more like magazines. And so magazines, in their turn, deprived of their staple formula of being the first to discuss, investigate and interview, suffered too.

The cinema changed totally in character. With the notable exception of a few, film stars became a distant memory; epics like *Star Wars*, *The Godfather* or *Jaws* could still draw huge queues, but anything unexceptional failed totally. People owning videos could hire a film within months of its release and watch it at home without any further expense or effort.

Television, however, brought the Open University into Britain's homes, which meant thousands of people every year could study, extend their horizons and qualify in fields they could never have otherwise entered.

Violence became one of the ugliest and yet apparently accepted faces of films and, to a degree, television. People seemed inoculated against it and watch appalling scenes in such horrors as *Apocalypse Now* and *Clockwork Orange* while they munched their popcorn. The television satellite stations meant, furthermore, that we could all watch men land on the moon and our world leaders assassinated in between making cups of tea.

The most extraordinary thing of all about the new world we live in is that we find so much of it ordinary.

WOMEN'S LOT

In the last quarter-century women have won their place in the world. They can now choose the course of their careers and the pattern of their lives; they can have one child, none or many; can marry or not, divorce if they wish; earn as much as men, enjoy the same power and the same status.

Many women today work outside the home, mothers included, and yet every time a survey is carried out we hear that women still do the lioness's share of shopping, cooking, housework and child-minding.

In spite of the advantages of improved contraception, better education and automation (removing physical strength as a qualification for most jobs) there was still prejudice against women. They were regarded as sex objects – a view to which their own sexual behaviour in the Sixties had possibly contributed.

They became more serious, organized and militant in the Seventies; demanding true equality in law, not mere gestures in its direction. They fought and slowly demolished the old prejudices about emotionalism and unreliability as they advanced. The Equal Opportunities Act passed in 1975 was an important milestone in women's history, and the legalization of abortion in 1967 and the Divorce Reform Act in 1971 both also did an enormous amount to free women.

There are women prime ministers, women judges, priests, professors and captains of industry. The quantity is still small. But the quality is undeniable. . .

OPPOSITE PAGE
Videos mean that films can be watched at home within months of their release.

RIGHT
Wide-eyed and long-legged: Twiggy immortalized the Sixties' dolly-bird look.

DRESSED FOR IT

Fashion has completely changed in character during the last twenty-five years. It is still a huge industry, earning vast amounts of money and accounting for a great deal of emotional, intellectual and creative endeavour. But the rules have changed.

Women are now fashion's masters, rather than its slaves. It carries on dictating, but only a few people do exactly what it says. The rest, encouraged by an increased self-confidence,

individuality and a genuine resistance to being told what to do, wear their own fashions, interpreting the season's rules and regulations in their own way. It is now perfectly possible to wear any one of a dozen looks and remain fashionable. The day of the autocratic designer, drilling the rise and fall of the hemline with military precision, is over. The best designers make clothes that can be worn stylishly for years. A St Laurent, a Jean Muir, a Burberry, do not date. It is a charming and comfortable age in which to wear clothes.

Yet in 1960 fashion tyranny was immense. Women of every size and age and with every shape of leg, hitched their skirts thigh-high and tried to look like Dolly Birds. The immortals of the decade were Jean Shrimpton and Twiggy, but a mass of beauties (Catherine Deneuve, Veruschka, Julie Christie), long-legged, huge-eyed and with clouds of blonde hair, wore the Sixties look, a curious blend of heart-stopping sensuality and schoolgirlishness, with extraordinary uniformity. Skirts were extremely short; hair and eyelashes were extremely long. Dresses were scarcely shaped, skimming the body briefly from neck to thigh. If hair wasn't long, it was carved into a sculptured bob.

ABOVE RIGHT AND RIGHT
Peace and love: flower power blossomed in the late Sixties.

OPPOSITE PAGE
A fairytale come true: one of the most popular heroines of the Eighties is the Princess of Wales.

Boots went thigh high. Jeans had wide flared bottoms and agonizingly tight tops. Fur coats were still socially acceptable. At couture level, Courreges and Ungaro put women into white gaberdine, sculptured shifts, white boots and, in the evening, silver-sequined trousers.

Paco Rabanne took women into the space age with dresses made of small plastic tiles; Pierre Cardin literally hung dresses from ring collars. Tired of all this little girlishness, the end of the decade saw Romance with multi-coloured full-skirted dresses, heavily embroidered with feathers and beads, and flounce upon flounce of lace; shirred and frilled leather, and long, high-wayman coats. Flower power and the pre-Raphaelites combined to make a new look alto-gether, and a much more womanly fantasy. Skirts began to fall, and at the same time shorts, in the guise of hot-pants, made a startling appearance.

With the less confident, less pushy feel of the Seventies and the rush back to the land came a clutch of 'peasant' clothes: layer upon layer of smocks and skirts in cotton or wool; knits, tweeds, and of course the Laura Ashley fantasy, of flouncy flowered prints, huge hats and perpetual summer picnics. Jean Muir, in con-trast, sculpted jersey skin-close in navy blue.

The Biba look – the stylish sexy Thirties shape, all sequins and satins, crushed velvet and little skull caps – swept London; in more realistic mood, skirts settled at mid-calf; Viyella shirts, cricket sweaters and wide trousers made yet another comeback, and velvet jackets hung in every wardrobe.

Annie Hall's influence was enormous; loose, comfortable and slightly crumpled, Diane Keaton's clothes hung on her like a witty remark. And towards the end of the Seventies the Punks made their entrance in clashing crude colours and leather zips and studs. What was originally anti-fashion became ironically Establishment and was worn in the smartest restaurants and clubs in London.

Hair had to be curled. The perm, long, shaggy, unstyled, was everywhere. Make-up was smudge eyed, glossy lipped. The new heroines were not set-piece clones but less perfect people: Lauren Hutton, Marisa Berenson, Meryl Streep.

Now in the mid-Eighties, clothes have grown up again. Casual clothes have panache: the crushed cotton Pacific jumpsuits, the Norma Kamali sweatshirt dresses, the endless inventive-ness of denim. Tailored clothes have class: Jasper Conran and Margaret Howell's fluid suits and dresses set the tone; and these lines are adapted and sold in today's chic coordinated retail outlets. Evening clothes are pure fantasy; the Emanuels or Bruce Oldfield leading the way into frills and furbelows or shimmering silken sheaths, making women look like heroines, and following the greatest fairytale heroine of this decade, the Princess of Wales.

ON THE HOME FRONT

The kitchen has changed totally in character during this century. Not merely in its equipment, but what goes on within its walls.

Once a place for hard labour, the domain of women only, it is now the heart of the home, a place to talk and meet and entertain, as well as eat and drink. The hard labour has been reduced by the pressing of buttons. The mid-Eighties kitchen could now contain a dishwasher, washing machine and tumble dryer, food processor, cooker, microwave, fridge, freezer, and wipe-clean work surfaces and floors.

Cooking has changed. For many the cumbersome everyday chore has become a quick knocking up of the daily meal, with intensive 'proper' cooking done only in the form of baking, bulk cooking for the freezer, or for parties or dinner parties. Partly because of the emphasis on eating more natural foods, and the benefit of raw vegetables and salads, families eat more simply and healthily, and the old days of stodgy foods seem like a calorific and exhausting nightmare. Science has been on women's side.

Kitchens have also become immensely design-orientated. The look of the kitchen is as important as the food it produces. Custom built kitchens are the status symbols of the Eighties; there are now couturiers of the kitchen as well as fashion. Built-in ovens housed in elaborate units, carefully carved and contoured wood, cupboards that slide, drawers that glide are all Eighties kitchen ingredients. Auto-timers, more reliable than they were initially, have revolutionized cooking for working women; self-cleaning ovens are standard, and no self respecting couture kitchen would have anything but a separate oven and hob. Then there are the culinary miracles, the microwaves, that cook a chicken in twenty minutes, bake a potato in five, and heat food up without drying it out. Freezers, hypermarkets and second cars keep shopping to a minimum.

The interest in food has grown tremendously; the nouvelle cuisine, the passion for French provincial cookery, the focus on natural goodness, have all combined to make people see food as something to take pleasure in rather than mere sustenance.

What all this means is that people can enjoy cooking and see it as a creative and pleasurable occupation rather than an onerous daily chore. And in the preparation of pleasurable food, the mighty Cube has always played no small part. . .

ABOVE
Today the look of the kitchen is
almost as important as the food
produced in it.

RIGHT
The microwave oven, culinary
miracle of the times.

THE ESSENTIAL INGREDIENT

OXO has always, from its earliest beginnings, been a part of history; during the Sixties and Seventies it went a few steps further and made history of its own.

The Sixties was the decade when the media took people over. Nobody could have foreseen how television seized the public imagination and created a whole new culture with a huge and dazzling cast of heroes and heroines. Oxo was not an also-ran in this field; it was out there, leading the race.

What Oxo did was create a new element in the culture – the first television commercial character with a life of her own, whose roots were solemnly discussed, whose upwardly mobile lifestyle was studied, whose domestic dramas formed an essential part of the nation's viewing life, and who became so real, so believable that people wrote to her in thousands to congratulate her on her successes, commiserate with her in her difficulties, to share their own problems with her – and to tut over her husband's bad manners at the table. This was Katie, the sparkling, almost unflappable heroine of the kitchen drama, cooking, serving and smiling over delicious meals, against such outrageous odds as the boss turning up for dinner with only thirty minutes' warning, and a small supper guest who didn't like stews.

Katie was not the only good thing that has happened to Oxo during the last quarter-century; the Company adjusted with style and flair to the dazzling pacey new world of the mini, the pop star and the Man on the Moon. It had always been one of its strengths that it could recognize, acknowledge and capitalize on the best of the

Almost unflappable: Katie, the heroine of the Oxo kitchen drama.

new while maintaining the strength of the old; it continued to associate itself with such eternal virtues as courage, good health and the spirit of adventure even while it shed its slightly folksy image and streamlined itself for entry into the foolhardy new world.

TAKING A BITE AT IT

One of the more dramatic departures from what might be called the Stock Market was the production of a potato crisp. Oxo joined forces with Rank Hovis McDougall and produced Chipmunk Crisps (no longer an Oxo product), with the only talking chipmunk in the world to do the selling

for them, in what was the heaviest television campaign *ever* for a crisp. Aimed primarily at children and sold in school canteens, zoos and Woburn Abbey, Chipmunk pushed itself hard with big promotions based on the ephemera so beloved by children: masks, badges and toys.

The other big event, timed to coincide with Oxo's Golden Jubilee, was the launch of Golden Oxo (later called Chicken Oxo), a lighter coloured and flavoured cube to use with chicken, pork and veal. This was a huge success, producing in due course the wickedly witty slogan 'Nine out of ten chickens prefer Oxo'.

In 1968, the parent Company merged with Brooke Bond, prompting predictable headlines about brewing beef tea, and a new food giant was created, with Oxo as one of its leading products.

Your very good health: the Chairmen of Liebig's Extract of Meat Co. and Brook Bond & Co. Ltd. drink to their companies' merger in 1968.

OXO ANON

A curious little item appeared in the *Daily Mirror* in November 1967. The Breathalyzer test had just hit the country, causing panic among drivers who liked a drink. A story was going round the Stock Exchange that Oxo shares should be snapped up because the company had solved the breathalyzer problem: an Oxo cube slipped into your last glass of gin (they said) would result in Oxogin. Ouch.

A year later, an equally odd tribute was made to Oxo by the Chichester Festival Theatre, no less, when they staged Thornton Wilder's *The Skin of Our Teeth*. A maidservant (played by that Sixties satire heroine Millicent Martin) emerged from the atomic shelter after a nuclear explosion and asked permission to go to a survival dance. On being told she had no money she produced a packet of Oxo cubes and declared that they would be accepted as hard currency anywhere. The original screenplay actually cited beef cubes, but the production manager thought Oxo cubes were 'the most instantly recognisable product in the field to the British public'.

OXO IN SERVICE

The newly liberated young housewife found herself under fire and the centre of attention early in the Sixties. Enjoying her freedom and adopting a slightly less devoted and earnest approach to her cookery, she was on the receiving end of a lot of criticism from the National Federation of Meat Traders. They said she wasn't spending enough time or trouble choosing the right meat and using the right recipes, but was spending too much money on expensive cuts. The Meat Traders got together with Oxo to launch a national series of lectures and demonstrations, the aim being to instruct the housewife in the value and use of cheaper cuts and to tell her week by week the best buy, with a recipe for cooking it.

This was a wild success. Throughout the Sixties and Seventies, the Oxo Home Economists travelled the country by train, with their Meat Budget Cookery Service, stopping off at halls and ballrooms everywhere. Local master butchers took part as well, and over 20,000 people attended during one twelve-week tour alone. It was an ingenious idea; and another piece of pioneering on Oxo's behalf. Not only did it help promote the cheaper cuts of meat and Oxo, it also genuinely brought new culinary ideas to the kitchen and the table.

Towards the end of the prosperous Sixties, the word 'Budget' was dropped from the title, and all types of meat cookery were demonstrated and discussed – including some much more exotic examples.

OXO IN PRINT

In 1961 the Oxo *Book of Meat Cookery* went into print – and nearly a million kitchens. Written by Bee Neilson, with assistance from the Master Butchers, it eventually outsold Mrs Beeton. It was not on sale in bookshops, but was obtainable direct from the Company or at the cookery demonstrations. In due course it became a reference book in many schools, no doubt indoctrinating embryonic young housewifes in the Oxo tradition.

The Book of Meat Cookery, Oxo's classic cookbook.

And here's a must for every kitchen

200 recipes on all kinds of meat and poultry incorporating sections on soups, sauces and stuffings · Carving charts · Illustrated pages · Descriptions of various cuts of meat and their uses · A section on wine · An ABC of meat cookery containing an illustrated list of useful equipment and a glossary of kitchen knowledge.

Price 10/6
(while stocks of this printing last)

The Book of Meat Cookery

Obtainable from Brooke Bond Oxo Limited, Leon House, High Street, Croydon, Surrey. CR9 1JQ

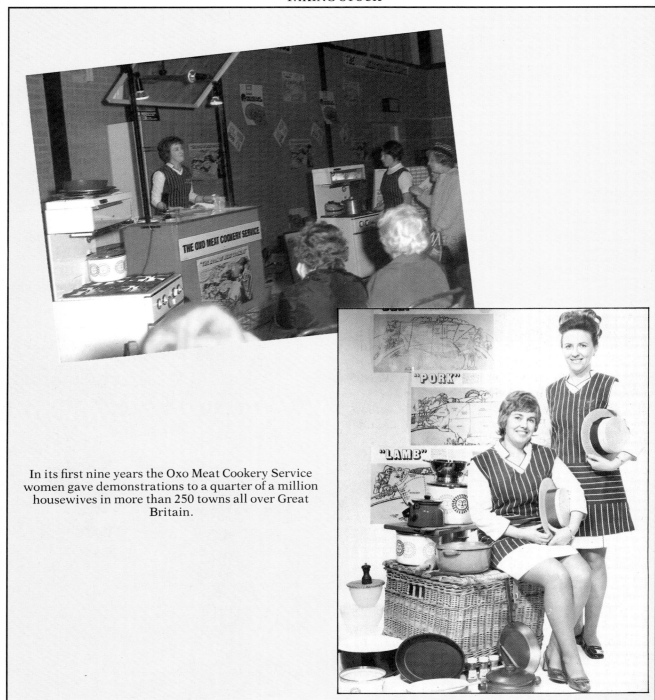

In its first nine years the Oxo Meat Cookery Service women gave demonstrations to a quarter of a million housewives in more than 250 towns all over Great Britain.

A PINT OF BEEFINESS

Oxo has always produced memorabilia, (collectors' items) from its earliest days. One of the most unusual was unearthed in the cellar of a hotel in Shropshire in 196 . It was a copper urn, in the form of a model of the Eddystone lighthouse, with the Oxo brand name on it. The most creative imaginations would have been hard-pressed to guess its use: quite large numbers of them were produced in the Twenties and used by caterers to serve Oxo in pubs at halfpenny a tot.

The Oxo heroes struggled on during this period: a non-stop walking champion Michael Potter, who walked for fifty-eight hours, was fed with soup and Oxo, Chay Blyth took the cube round the world with him, and Donald Ridler took it across the Atlantic in his one-man, makeshift, home-made sailing boat. Donald Crowhurst improved his diet and his chances of winning the *Sunday Times* Round the World Golden Globe sailing race in 1968. Oxo sponsored Mr Crowhurst by supplying him with innumerable tins of Fray Bentos corned beef and enough cubes to feed a fleet. The pioneering spirit of Oxo, like that of Dr Liebig, was very much alive.

MASS MARKETING

An extremely significant piece of social change took place during this period. The pattern of shopping altered absolutely. There were fewer cosy corner shops, with their caring service, personal touch and high prices. In (along with the working wife and the massively increased use of the motor car) came the supermarket, with its high-speed shopping, economy offers and its element of impulse buying. Oxo had to change its charmingly folksy tins for some snappy new packaging, and to involve itself in very competitive marketing, in the way of on-pack offers and giveaways.

PUTTING IT ABOUT

By the mid-Sixties, highly sophisticated sales promotions were becoming commonplace. Oxo did not lag behind in this particular race. A company of American sales promotion consultants helped perfect a hugely complex and catchy competition, with such lavish prizes as

Katie's girls featured in Sixties' Oxo promotion campaigns.

Capable Katie: played by Mary Holland, she was a young housewife who was competent, attractive and a bit sexy. As well as appearing on Oxo television commercials, she also made real-life appearances.

cars, dishwashers and cine cameras. Noughts and Crosses had always been felt a natural platform for an Oxo competition, but there was a considerable problem in getting quite a large amount of necessary wordage on to the extremely small space of an Oxo pack. Oxo, being the company it was, made it. The competition was a wild success, promoted heavily on television and commercial radio, and by banners on fleets of cars.

There were other hard-sell promotions: a balloon race (*prizes*, 100 cars) 'spot the Oxo shopper' (*prize*, one car) and a bingo-style affair that had to be frozen before a single eye went down because of a High Court decision against a similar contest.

A more respectable business altogether was Oxo's involvement in the Great Schools Contest, a heavily educational promotion inviting school children to submit a project on the Alcock and Brown first transatlantic flight (on which of course they were accompanied by The Cube).

KITCHEN STOVE HEROINE

All this, however, paled into insignificance with the birth of Katie.

She first saw the light of day in 1958, but it was a year or so before the nation took her to their hearts and made her a part of their own families. Mary Holland, who played Katie for eighteen years, says that she still gets recognized every day of her life. 'People say, "Oh, it's Katie, isn't it?" or "How's your little boy?"'

Katie was the brainchild of Oxo's advertising team at J. Walter Thompson. The product needed a new, more successful image – in advertising jargon, to be upgraded socially. Katie did it for them.

The idea of having a young housewife, with exactly the right lifestyle (not too low, not too high), attractive, competent and also a touch sexy, was an inspiration. It is hard to imagine now that television has become so sophisticated, how extraordinarily powerful and persuasive such a person could be – given that she was believable.

Katie was believable. Absolutely, 100 per cent, 22 carat, through and through believable. So carefully was she characterized that every detail of her life – right down to her husband Philip's job and their car and the way he travelled to work each day, their joint aspirations and their social life – was endlessly discussed. Before she was christened a shortlist of thirty names was under consideration.

Katie had to be competent, charming and a good manager; there was enough money for dinner parties (especially the kind where she entertained the boss), but making meat go further was very much a part of her and Oxo's job.

Katie was an old-style wife (hardly surprising in the early Sixties) intent on keeping her man happy. The sign off 'Oxo gives a meal man appeal' was as crucial to the series as Katie's dazzling smile and Philip's hearty appetite.

Katie first went out on the screen wondering what to give Philip for his supper. Two commercials later showed him merely appreciating whatever it was she cooked him. Then the Agency did some surveys. Nothing at all had happened; sales stayed static and nobody had noticed Katie.

But by February 1960 she had taken off and soon she was a star in her own right. The commercials became more dramatically ambitious. She and Philip went out for picnics, entertained the boss, had a child, moved to the country, went to America, even had the odd tiff. The audience loved them. And Oxo. As Katie grew in popularity and believability, so the sales of Oxo increased.

Her phenomenal believability was due in a

considerable degree to the skill of the actress who played her. Mary Holland (whose previous parts had included Little Lord Fauntleroy's mother) said that initially she and Katie were not the same people at all. 'She was terribly proper, much more so than I was. In the late Fifties people were beginning to relax and be more as they are now. It was the beginning of live and let live. I did feel Katie was a little bit of a throwback at the beginning. But after the first couple of years, she did become more relaxed, more like me. It was certainly the first of the sexy commercials. I didn't think of myself as a particularly sexy person, but I was certainly the first person on television, for instance, not to wear a roll-on girdle. Everybody else did. So we did break new ground, I mean her bottom *wiggled*. And by 1968 I really felt she had caught up with me. After that she wore the sort of clothes I did. In fact she wore lots of my own clothes.'

Katie didn't just appear on television, she made real life appearances opening supermarkets (along with husband Philip, growing slowly more portly after years of Katie's cooking). And wherever they went, people bombarded her with questions about her son David's schooling, and how she'd found America.

Once in one commercial when Philip spoke sharply to Katie, all the girls in an electronics factory came out on strike. When he used a hunk of bread to mop up his gravy, thousands of people complained it was bad manners. When Katie started cooking the minute her shopping basket touched the kitchen table, her fans started tutting because she didn't wash her hands first.

Katie's fan mail was considerable; half of it from men. The way she combined culinary skills with her own undeniable man appeal was one of the series' more remarkable qualities. She was pretty and sexy and charming, which men liked, and vulnerable, which women liked even more. When she talked too much about her baby or

GIVES A MEAL MAN APPEAL

cooked food Philip didn't like, the female hearts of the country went out to her. The whole thing was an advertising and marketing triumph. It turned a sales pitch into a dramatic series, product promoters into flesh and blood people – and became part of the fabric of the social life of the Sixties and Seventies. It also – very importantly – sold an awful lot of Oxo cubes.

WAS THERE LIFE AFTER KATIE?

There was. In the end, after 18 years, even a paragon palls; and Katie was felt, finally, to have dated. 'As the personality promoting a product grows older, so does the brand,' said one of the Oxo advertising chaps a trifle brutally. Women who were in their cradles when Katie first started adding man appeal to meals were now in the kitchen.

The Man Appeal slogan stayed, but the new symbol of the product in the public's mind was a pair of fingers doing the Oxo Crumble. That was on posters. On television men who were beefy and believable talked about their wives' cooking. Dennis Waterman of *The Sweeney* was the first famous face to take over from Katie. He was seen opening letters from his mum, urging him to eat well with the help of the new beefier cube. Their numbers swelled to twelve with the Oxo Man of the Month Calendar.

Oxo men weren't just macho. They played with their children, rescued kittens from trees and remained cheerful while walking home in the

OPPOSITE PAGE
The famous crumble: a pair of fingers doing the Oxo crumble became the new symbol of the product.

ABOVE RIGHT AND RIGHT
Man appeal: Dennis Waterman was the first famous face to take over from Katie. He and others featured on the Oxo Man of the Month calendar.

pouring rain (admittedly to an Oxo supper). All this took place to the accompaniment of a particularly catchy jingle recorded by the Guys and Dolls called 'Only Oxo Does It' and eventually released as a single.

It was all very catchy and clever. But somehow the ghost of Katie hung around the Oxo kitchen. She hasn't come back to it. But her successor is there – with a more harrassed husband and a worse behaved family. Lynda Bellingham plays her with a sexy wit, and she certainly doesn't wear a girdle either.

Guys and Dolls sang the catchy advertising jingle in the late Seventies' Oxo television commercials.

REAL FAMILY LIFE

The point about the new Oxo family is that it is presented showing the real ups and the downs of family life, which is a novelty in a television commercial. The children shout and squabble and send up their parents. The parents row and sometimes don't speak at all and occasionally share a sexy memory or two over the supper table. It's all very reassuring and human and funny and fun. Research showed that the perfect behaviour of perfect television people makes real people feel very imperfect indeed. Research also showed that the housewife was a 'tense vulnerable figure at the centre of a highly pressured environment'. Most housewives will recognize themselves like that, rather than as the calm competent creature who swans round most television commercials.

Lynda Bellingham speaks for millions of real life counterparts when she says the new Mrs Oxo 'isn't well organized but she means well ...' 'She's hassled, but active and outgoing,' says Oxo. Her family doesn't swoon appreciatively over her cooking, nor even take much notice of it half the time. But the food always improves matters (as it does in real life) and Oxo is once again selling itself brilliantly and convincingly.

And breaking entirely new advertising ground as it does so.

ABOVE
Into the Eighties: actress Lynda Bellingham first played mum in the Oxo advertisements screened in October 1983.
RIGHT
The new Oxo family shows the real ups and downs of family life.

RECIPES

DURING the past twenty-five years, new technology has entered the kitchen in many forms, which has transformed the busy cook's role. Food has changed, too – travelling abroad, as many people now do, has given anyone keen on cooking the chance to acquire an international cuisine.

At the beginning of this period, in 1961, Oxo's most famous cookery book, containing a wide variety of interesting recipes, was launched. It was called *The Book of Meat Cookery*, and outsold Mrs Beeton. Some of the recipes given here have been selected from this book and its successor, *The New Book of Meat Cookery*.

BOEUF EN DAUBE

Make this classic French dish the day before it is required and chill it overnight. The fat can be removed easily before re-heating.

SERVES 4–6

1½lb (675g) stewing steak
4oz (100g) piece of unsmoked, streaky bacon
½pt (300ml) inexpensive red wine
4 tbs oil
¾lb (350g) carrots, sliced
¾lb (350g) onions, sliced
1 clove of garlic, crushed
1 rounded tbs tomato purée
1 red Oxo cube dissolved in ¾pt (450ml) hot water
1½ level tsp salt
black pepper
1 bay leaf
1 sprig of parsley

Trim any excess fat from the meat and cut it into neat 1in (2.5cm) cubes. Trim off the rind and any bone from the bacon and cut the lean meat into strips. Put the meat and bacon in a large bowl and pour over the wine. Cover and leave in a cool place to marinate for several hours. When the meat is ready, heat the oven to 300°F, 150°C, gas mark 2. Heat the oil in a frying pan, lift the meat from the marinade and fry quickly to brown. Lift it out with a slotted spoon and put in a heatproof casserole about 4½pt (2.5l) in capacity. Add the vegetables and garlic to the pan and fry for 2 to 3 minutes. Lift them out and add to the casserole with the meat. Put the marinade, tomato purée, Oxo stock, salt, pepper, bay leaf and parsley in the frying pan and bring to the boil, stirring constantly. Pour into the casserole, cover with a lid or foil and cook in the oven for 3 to 4 hours or until the beef is tender. Taste and check seasoning. Remove the bayleaf and parsley before serving.

SAVOURY PANCAKES

SERVES 4

FILLING
2 streaky bacon rashers, chopped
1lb (450g) minced beef
1 onion, chopped
1 stick of celery, chopped
1 level tsp plain flour
1 red Oxo cube dissolved in ¼pt (150ml) hot water
2 level tbs tomato purée
1 level tsp salt
black pepper

SAUCE
1oz (25g) butter or margarine
1oz (25g) plain flour
½pt (300ml) milk
½ level tsp made English mustard
salt and pepper
4oz (100g) Cheddar cheese, grated

8 plain pancakes
1 sprig of parsley

First prepare the filling. Place the bacon, beef, onion and celery in a saucepan and cook gently for 5 to 10 minutes. Stir in the flour, add the Oxo stock and bring to the boil, stirring constantly. Add all the remaining ingredients for the filling, cover with a lid or foil and simmer for 30 to 40 minutes or until tender. Meanwhile make the sauce. Melt the butter or margarine in a small saucepan, stir in the flour and cook for 1 minute. Blend in the milk and bring to the boil, stirring until thickened. Simmer for 2 minutes. Add the mustard, salt, pepper and 3oz (75g) of the cheese. Stir until the cheese has melted. Spread the pancakes flat and divide the meat mixture between them. Roll them up, arrange in a single layer in a shallow heatproof dish and keep warm. Spoon over the cheese sauce and sprinkle with the remaining cheese. Cook under a moderate grill until the top is golden brown and bubbling. Garnish with the parsley and serve immediately.

EASY BEEF PIE

This dish is ideal for storing in the freezer and equally tasty eaten hot or cold.

SERVES 6

FILLING
1 level tbs cornflour
1 red Oxo cube
4 tbs water
¾lb (350g) minced beef
1 small onion, grated
4oz (100g) carrots, grated
½ level tsp dried mixed herbs
salt and pepper

PASTRY
8oz (225g) plain flour
2oz (50g) margarine
2oz (50g) lard
about 2 tbs cold water
sprigs of parsley to garnish

Heat the oven to 400°F, 200°C, gas mark 6. Put the cornflour, crumbled Oxo cube and water in a bowl. Stir until blended and smooth, add all the remaining filling ingredients and mix thoroughly. Make the pastry. Put the flour in a bowl, cut the margarine and lard into small pieces and rub in the flour with the fingertips until the mixture resembles fine breadcrumbs. Add sufficient water to mix to a firm dough. Roll out about two-thirds of the pastry on a lightly floured surface and use it to line a deep metal pie plate or flan ring 8in (20cm) in diameter. Place the filling in the pastry case, then roll out the remaining pastry. Dampen the edges of this piece of pastry and cover the top of the pie with it. Seal the edges securely and make a small slit in the centre to allow the steam to escape. Brush the pie-top with a little milk to glaze. Bake in the oven for 50 to 60 minutes or until the pastry is golden brown. Garnish with sprigs of parsley.

SWEETHEART SURPRISE

This delicious recipe was featured in one of the Oxo family TV advertisements, and makes an unusual surprise for someone special on Valentine's Day.

SERVES 4

1½lb braising steak
3 tbs flour (seasoned with salt and pepper)
oil
12 button onions, peeled
2 carrots, peeled and cut into strips
1 red pepper, deseeded and sliced
1 red Oxo cube dissolved in ¾pt (450ml) hot water
1 tbs tomato purée
1½ tbs french mustard
slices of bread
oil for frying
freshly chopped parsley

Cut the meat into cubes and coat it in seasoned flour. Heat the oil and fry the meat until browned then transfer it to a casserole. Lightly fry the onions, carrots and pepper in the same pan. Stir in the remaining seasoned flour then add the Oxo stock, tomato purée and mustard. Pour over the beef. Cover and cook in an oven at 325°F, 160°C, gas mark 3 for approximately 1 hour. Shortly before serving cut heart shapes from the slices of bread and fry them in oil until golden brown. Serve the casserole sprinkled with parsley and the heart-shaped croutons.

AMERICAN SPARE RIBS

A great out-of-doors dish, but make sure you have plenty of paper napkins handy.

SERVES 4

2 tbs oil
12oz (350g) onions, chopped
2 cloves of garlic, crushed
4 tbs vinegar
2½oz (62g) can of tomato purée
¼ tsp chilli powder
6 tbs clear honey
2 red Oxo cubes dissolved in ½pt (300ml) hot water
2½lb (1.1kg) pork ribs
salt and black pepper

Heat the oven to 375°F, 190°C, gas mark 5. Heat the oil in a large saucepan, add the onions and fry gently for 10 to 15 minutes or until pale golden brown and soft. Add all the remaining ingredients except the ribs and bring to the boil, stirring constantly. Simmer uncovered for 10 minutes. Arrange the ribs in a single layer in a shallow heatproof dish, season with salt and pepper and pour over half the sauce. Cook in the oven for 45 minutes. Remove from the oven and drain off the surplus fat or blot with kitchen paper. Coat with the remaining sauce and roast for a further 15 to 30 minutes or until golden brown and tender.

PORK 'N' PEACHES

Peaches make a change from the usual apple sauce. Use spiced peaches for a superb party dish.

SERVES 4

15oz (411g) can of peach halves
cold water
2 level tbs cornflour
¼ level tsp ground ginger
1 tbs vinegar
1 tbs soy sauce
1 chicken Oxo cube
4 pork chops, steaks or slices
butter
1oz (25g) browned, flaked almonds
½ small green pepper, cut into rings

Drain the peaches, reserving the syrup and making it up to ½pt (300ml) with cold water. Place the cornflour in a small saucepan with the ginger, stir in the vinegar, soy sauce, crumbled Oxo cube and peach syrup and bring to the boil, stirring constantly until the sauce has thickened. Simmer for 3 minutes. Heat the grill to moderate. Trim off any excess fat or rind from the pork. Place the peaches in the bottom of the grill pan, under the rack; arrange the pork on top of the rack, dot with a little butter and cook for 15 to 20 minutes or until the pork is tender, turning them once. Lift out the meat, place on a warm serving dish and arrange the peaches on top. Add the juices from the grill pan to the sauce and heat through. Taste and check seasoning. Spoon the sauce over the pork, sprinkle with the almonds and green pepper rings and serve immediately.

PORK HONGROISE

The soured cream makes this a rather rich dish. The pork can be served arranged on a bed of rice or pasta for a party, with the soured cream poured over the top.

SERVES 4–6

1½lb (675g) pork fillet or boned loin of pork
2 tbs oil
1 onion, chopped
1 level tsp paprika pepper
½oz (12½g) plain flour
½pt (300ml) water
1 chicken Oxo cube
5 tbs sherry
1 level tsp tomato purée
salt and pepper
6oz (175g) small button mushrooms
½oz (12g) cornflour
2 tbs cold water
¼pt (150ml) carton of soured cream

Cut the pork into 1½in (3.5cm) pieces. Heat the oil in a saucepan and quickly fry the pork pieces until they are just beginning to brown. Remove them from the pan and drain on kitchen paper. Add the onion and paprika pepper to the pan and fry for 2 minutes. Remove the pan from the heat, blend in the flour and cook for 1 minute. Stir in the water, crumbled Oxo cube, sherry and tomato purée, return to the heat and bring to the boil, stirring constantly until the sauce has thickened. Season well and add the meat. Cover with a lid or foil and simmer for about 40 minutes or until the pork is tender. At the end of the cooking time, add the whole mushrooms. Blend the cornflour to a smooth paste with the water, add to the pan and bring to the boil. Just before serving, stir in the soured cream or turn into a warm serving dish and spoon the soured cream on top. Serve immediately, with rice or pasta.

COURGETTES WITH HAM

A very economical way of using up leftover bacon or ham.

SERVES 4

2oz (50g) butter or margarine
1½lb (675g) courgettes, washed and cut into ¼in (0.6cm) slices
4oz (100g) mushrooms, sliced
4–6oz (100–175g) lean ham, chopped

SAUCE
1½oz (40g) butter
1½oz (40g) plain flour
¾pt (450ml) milk
1 chicken Oxo cube
salt and pepper
3oz (75g) Cheddar cheese, grated

Melt the butter in a frying pan and fry the courgettes for 10 minutes, turning occasionally. Add the mushrooms and cook for a further 5 minutes, by which time the courgettes should have turned pale golden brown. Lift courgettes and mushrooms out with a slotted spoon and arrange in a shallow heatproof dish. Cover with the chopped ham. Meanwhile make the sauce. Melt the butter in a small saucepan, stir in the flour and cook for 2 minutes. Add the milk and bring to the boil, stirring until the sauce has thickened. Add the crumbled Oxo cube and stir until well blended. Taste and check seasoning. Heat the grill to hot. Spoon the sauce over the ham, sprinkle with the grated cheese and cook under the grill for 3 to 4 minutes or until the cheese is golden brown and bubbling. Serve immediately.

LAMB BOULANGÈRE

This famous French dish is named after the village baker who obligingly cooked a large leg of lamb in his oven for the housewife who did not have enough room in hers.

SERVES 6–8

1 small leg of lamb
2 cloves of garlic, peeled and cut into thin slivers
1 sprig of fresh rosemary
8oz (225g) onions, thinly sliced
1½lb (675g) potatoes, peeled and cut into thick slices
salt and pepper
1 red Oxo cube dissolved in ½pt (300ml) hot water
a little chopped parsley

Heat the oven to 375°F, 190°C, gas mark 5. Trim any excess fat from the lamb, press garlic slivers into the meat and tie the sprig of rosemary over it. Mix the onions and potatoes. Place them in a shallow heatproof dish, season and arrange the lamb on top. Pour Oxo stock over the meat and vegetables. Cover with foil and roast in the oven for 30 minutes per lb (450g) plus an extra 30 minutes. After the first hour remove the foil, baste the meat and vegetables and return them to the oven to continue cooking. When the meat is cooked, untie the rosemary and place a fresh sprig on top. Sprinkle the vegetables with chopped parsley and serve straight from the dish in which they were cooked.

SPICY LAMB

Despite its name this is not a hot dish; it has a mildly spicy taste which will appeal to all the family.

SERVES 4–6

1½lb (675g) boneless fillet, leg or shoulder of lamb
1½oz (40g) plain flour
2 level tsp mild curry powder
1½ level tsp salt
black pepper
2 tbs oil
1pt (600ml) water
2 chicken Oxo cubes
8oz (225g) button onions, peeled and left whole
8oz (225g) small carrots, quartered lengthways

Trim any excess fat from the lamb and cut the lean meat into 1in (2.5cm) cubes. Put the flour, curry powder, salt and pepper in a bag, add the lamb and shake well to coat it thoroughly. Heat the oil in a saucepan, add the lamb and fry for 2 to 3 minutes. Stir in the remaining flour, add the water and crumbled Oxo cubes and bring to the boil, stirring constantly. Add the onions and carrots, cover with a lid and simmer very gently for about 1¼ hours or until the lamb and vegetables are tender. Taste and check seasoning. Turn into a warm dish and serve immediately.

RABBIT SWEET 'N' SOUR

Rabbit is easily obtainable fresh or frozen and is very tasty and tender. It is suitable for slow cooking.

SERVES 4

2 tsp soy sauce
¼pt (150ml) vinegar
2 tbs brown sugar
1lb (675g) rabbit joints
2 tbs oil
1 chicken Oxo cube dissolved in ½pt (300ml) hot water
2½ tbs cornflour
1 red and 1 green pepper, seeded and sliced
2oz (50g) sultanas
parsley for garnish

Blend the soy sauce, vinegar and brown sugar together and marinade the rabbit in this for 1 to 2 hours then drain, reserving the marinade. Heat the oil and fry the meat until golden brown; drain and place in a casserole. Pour off the excess oil from the pan. Blend the cornflour with a little cold water and add with the marinade to the Oxo stock. Pour into the pan and bring to the boil, stirring. Add the peppers and pour the mixture over the rabbit joints. Cover and cook in an oven preheated to 325°F, 160°C, gas mark 3 for about 2 hours. Add the sultanas 15 minutes before the end of the cooking time. Sprinkle the dish with parsley to serve.

CHICKEN AND ALMOND BAKE

SERVES 4

4 chicken joints
oil
1 chicken Oxo cube dissolved in ¼pt (150ml) hot water
4 thick slices bread
fat for frying
2 tsp cornflour
½ tsp dry mustard
3 tbs dry sherry
½oz (12g) slivered almonds, toasted

Secure the joints in neat shapes with cocktail sticks. Brush with oil and arrange in a single layer in ovenproof dish. Pour over the chicken stock. Bake uncovered at 375°F, 190°C, gas mark 5 for about 40 minutes. Using a 3½in (9cm) cutter, stamp out one round from each bread slice. Fry in shallow fat until golden brown; drain well. Remove the joints from the juices and keep hot. Blend the cornflour and mustard with the sherry, then pour into the bubbling juices, stirring. Arrange the chicken on the bread croûtes. Cover with the sauce and sprinkle with almonds. Serve with baked tomatoes and peas to make a colourful dish.

CHINESE CHICKEN

This recipe could be made with fillet of pork, prawns or shrimps instead of chicken.

SERVES 4

12oz (350g) breast of chicken
12oz (350g) white cabbage
6 spring onions
2 level tsp cornflour
2 tbs sherry
2 tbs corn oil
salt and black pepper
1 green pepper, seeded and thinly sliced
8oz (225g) bean sprouts
1 clove of garlic, crushed
1 chicken Oxo cube dissolved in ¼pt (150ml) hot water
2 tbs soy sauce

Slice the chicken into fine pencil-thin strips about 2in (5cm) long. Shred the cabbage finely. Cut the spring onions into 2in (5cm) lengths. Blend the cornflour with the sherry. Heat the oil in a wok or large heavy saucepan until very hot. Season the chicken, add to the pan and cook over fierce heat for 1 minute, constantly tossing and moving the chicken about the pan. Lift it out with a slotted spoon and arrange on a plate. Reheat the wok or pan and add the cabbage, green pepper, bean sprouts, spring onions and garlic. Cook for 3 to 4 minutes, tossing constantly. Return the chicken to the pan. Add the Oxo stock to the pan with the soy sauce and blended cornflour. Cook for at least 1 minute or until the liquid is creamy and the vegetables are still crisp. Taste and check seasoning. Serve with rice.

INDEX